A TRUE STORY OF CRIME, FAITH AND FAMILY

PURSUED

DONALD SMARTO

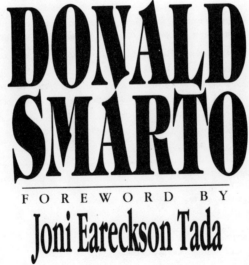

FOREWORD BY
Joni Eareckson Tada

INTERVARSITY PRESS
DOWNERS GROVE, ILLINOIS 60515

InterVarsity Press is the book-publishing division of InterVarsity Christian Fellowship, a student movement active on campus at hundreds of universities, colleges and schools of nursing in the United States of America, and a member movement of the International Fellowship of Evangelical Students. For information about local and regional activities, write Public Relations Dept., InterVarsity Christian Fellowship, 6400 Schroeder Rd., P.O. Box 7895, Madison, WI 53707-7895.

Distributed in Canada through InterVarsity Press, 860 Denison St., Unit 3, Markham, Ontario L3R 4H1, Canada.

All Scripture quotations, unless otherwise indicated, are from the Holy Bible, New International Version. Copyright © *1973, 1978, International Bible Society. Used by permission of Zondervan Bible Publishers.*

ISBN 0-8308-1717-4

Printed in the United States of America ∞

Library of Congress Cataloging-in-Publication Data
Smarto, Donald.
    Pursued: a true story of crime, faith, and family/Donald
Smarto.
        p.   cm.
    ISBN 0-8308-1717-4
    1. Smarto, Donald.   2. Christian biography—United
States.
    3. Converts—United States—Biography.   I. Title.
    BR1725.S46863A3   1989
    209'.2—dc20
     [B]   *90-4200*
                                                          CIP

13   12   11   10   9   8   7   6   5   4   3   2   1
99   98   97   96   95   94   93   92   91   90

To Sig,
whose confidence
gave me wings.

Acknowledgments

Thanks to my friends Chuck Colson and Joni Eareckson Tada for encouraging me to share this story with a larger audience.

Thanks to Roger Palms, editor of *Decision* magazine, for sharing my testimony in his magazine in 1986.

Thanks to Bill Glass, my good friend, who has shared his wisdom regarding forgiveness.

My gratitude to Bob Harvey, my pastor, who has nurtured me in the faith with patience and love.

My appreciation to my dedicated secretary, Jude Skallerup, for her prayer support for this book.

Thanks to my editor, Don Stephenson, for refining the manuscript with his insightful questions.

Special thanks to my wife, Regina, and my son, Luke, for their loyalty and love.

Ultimate gratitude to God for his grace and pursuit.

Foreword

Reading *Pursued* is a lot like reading a mystery. Remember those Perry Mason stories? Not just the books but the old TV shows? Sure you do.

Usually, at the end of the program, we'd see the prosecuting attorney, Perry Mason's opponent, pounding the jury railing with his point of view. That attorney made his case seem so airtight, so logical. He not only convinced the jury, he usually swayed me too—that is, until it was Perry's turn to sum up.

Good old Perry Mason would rise, shuffle his papers and approach the jury. Before I knew it, he dismantled the so-called airtight arguments. He turned the whole case topsy-turvy, exposing the errors in what previously seemed to be true. In the final moments, I found myself exclaiming with the jury, "Ah-hah! Why didn't I see that all along? Now the truth is obvious!"

Don Smarto's story reads like a Perry Mason mystery.

Don's journey through error seemed so right to him at the time. The love of religion. The airtight arguments of church canons and creeds. His life was so convincingly . . . righteous. That is, to everyone but Don.

Somehow he sensed that God was pursuing him through a

path of error into the truth. And that's what *Pursued* is all about. As you read, the mystery will lead you from the halls of Mafia dons in Sicily to a quiet monastery near Kansas City, and on to the stench and violence of prison.

Hey, I love mysteries—maybe that's why I love this man's story. But I'll tell you why else I've enjoyed reading Don Smarto's journey from error into truth. I've been reminded that I, at times, am convinced too easily by the arguments of another prosecuting attorney . . . the devil. Our enemy tries to make an airtight argument on the side of religion, with all its traditional trappings. But God's the one with the real truth—he pursues a relationship with us.

We have yet to read the last page of Don Smarto's story. His mystery isn't over—and neither are ours. But one day the final chapters will be written. Christ, our advocate, will make clear every single fact. Each case will be closed, the gavel will sound—and all, like Don, will know that God is the Truth.

I'm so thankful to know he pursues us to that end.

Joni Eareckson Tada

Introduction

How I got to be a leader in the evangelical church is as much a mystery to me as I am sure it is to many. The overwhelming pressures of family and culture should have sent me in a very different direction.

As long as I can remember, I have always believed in God, although he seemed distant and austere. Jesus was another matter! I accepted his historical reality, but the image of the baby in the manger was a mystery, and the image of the man on the cross was an enigma. Yet I've sensed, even from childhood, that God was pursuing me, despite my dysfunctional family and my equally dysfunctional religious practices, which were to last more than half my life.

I grew up without a Bible and rarely attended church. I came to accept religious superstitions which were often more frightening than consoling. At home I witnessed violent quarelling, compulsive gambling and long-standing grudges rooted deep in Sicilian tradition. The world seemed hostile, a mirror of the problems in my own family. I retreated into another world, a world of religious legalism, which, though unhealthy, in many ways was logical and secure and stable. Yet God did not leave me there. He was never satisfied with the life I was building for myself. He pursued.

I confess I do not understand all of God's choices for my life, especially the ones that were harsh and painful, but I realize that even in small ways, he used those experiences to build my character, my patience, my perseverance and my ability to comfort others.

As I look back at my forty-plus years, my heart is overwhelmed to know that God has been always there, always faithful to me. At the same time, I'm confronted with the stark reality that I've been unfaithful to him.

In telling my story,* I have the benefit of any Monday-morning quarterback. It's easier to see my mistakes and the coach's wisdom from a distance. As I look back, I'm struck more by God's love than any sense of accomplishment on my part. I believe that God's power shows up best in our weakness. That is perhaps the only strength of my story.

This, then, is not an account of a person's triumph, but of struggle; not of security, but of searching; not of self-satisfaction, but of restlessness and suffering; not of spiritual superiority, but of weakness and slow growth.

If my story points to a very big God who constantly pursues us with his love, then I have succeeded.

---

*Out of respect for my family and friends, some of the names in this book have been changed.

Chapter 1

ANCESTORS

THERESA FIORINO, A WOMAN IN HER EARLY TWENTIES, WAS MENDing a torn garment in her modest, one-room apartment. That day in Marsala, Sicily, it was over ninety degrees by midday, a dry heat. The open shutters brought in dust and flies, the clatter of a horse and cart on the rough stone street below and the screams of a mother calling her child.

But the noise outside was drowned by a couple shouting in the downstairs apartment, as it had been many times before. Only this time the shouts were becoming louder and more intense. Then there were long pauses occasionally punctuated by staccato profanity.

The longer silence was suddenly interrupted by someone running up the stairs. The fighting couple burst into Theresa's room, the argument erupting once more. Before Theresa could comprehend what was happening, the women had grabbed a kitchen knife and stabbed her husband in the back. His face froze; his eyes bulged out with shock. He choked in the middle of a word and fell to the hard wooden floor, never to regain consciousness. The woman ran from the room, returning moments later with the carabinieri, the police. She pointed to Theresa and screamed, "Murderer! Murderer!"

News spread quickly through Marsala: Theresa Fiorino had been charged with murder—the motive jealousy. Carmella Fiorino, Theresa's sister, rushed home when the news reached the bakery where she worked; not trusting the courts for justice, the family would make their own plans quickly.

That night the Fiorino family bribed a policeman and brought Theresa to a conscripted boat which took her to the island of Tunis to live in exile. Theresa died ten years later, in 1896, never having seen her family again. Carmella never stopped mourning the loss of her sister, although she went on with her life, marrying and having a large family.

Carmella was my paternal grandmother.

I had neither an interest nor a knowledge of my ancestors until later in life. But to understand my story, you must understand my family's story. And Sicily is where it began. My grandparents and their ancestors were born in Marsala, Sicily. Their heritage and environment shaped their attitudes, their reasons for coming to America, the way they raised their children. My Sicilian upbringing shaped my life.

Italians are "habited by devils"—or so a sixteenth-century proverb says; some would say the Sicilians are habited by more than their fair share. In my grandparents' day, Sicilians could be stubborn, superstitious and bigoted, but their lives were also filled with love and laughter. All my ancestors were poor and struggling people. Most of the earth was dry clay and very poor for growing. The town of Marsala, on the west coast of Sicily, exported wine from its vineyards, and grapes are easy prey to poor growing conditions.

Sicilians are proud people, perhaps because they were oppressed by at least five other countries for centuries. By the time Garibaldi joined Sicily to Italy in 1860, the wealthy landowners neglected the basic needs of their own people. Exploitation and distrust of government and the law translated into close family solidarity.

The Mafia came out of these roots. They became the heroes and protectors of the poor.

In Marsala, the church stood in the center of town—and at the center of family celebrations. Perhaps because of their daily hardships, my ancestors used every occasion to celebrate life. They would go to the church for baptisms—to celebrate new life; for weddings—to celebrate a new way of life; and for funerals—to celebrate the memory of a life. Every church event was a cause for festivity, even first communion and confirmation.

My ancestors were emotional but also sensitive and comical. The same men who were inhibited in church embraced each other with hugs and kisses at the family gatherings that followed. Parties could last for days, with abundant wine and music. The guests danced with the fury typified by the tarantella, the native dance imitating a person who had been bitten by a tarantula.

My great-grandfathers on my mother's side were Vincenzo Titone and Frank Cappitelli. Vincenzo was born in Marsala in 1840 and worked as a barrel maker for the popular Marsala winery. Frank Cappitelli was born in 1852 and was a bricklayer. He and his wife, Rose, had fourteen children, of which only eight survived. His income was so small that his wife earned money by nursing babies for a local orphanage.

Vincenzo's wages as a barrel maker were meager as well. On holidays his wife, Josephine, would cook a piece of pork fat over a fire so the smell would carry into the courtyard. That way their neighbors would believe the Titones were having a feast even when they had no food.

These two families were united when Frank and Rose's son William, my maternal grandfather, married Vincenzo and Josephine's daughter, Santa.

Family traditions were very important in Sicily, and according to that tradition William asked Santa's parents for permission to marry. It was always customary to have a dinner afterward, so Josephine used the only ingredients she had, flour and tomatoes, to make a crude homemade pasta. Fortunately, her daughter Santa was destined to have an easier life.

William became a successful barber, but his sights were even higher than success in the gray hills of Sicily. With new immigration laws opening up the United States to Europeans, William sought the promise of America—a life of material prosperity and dignity.

William's older brother, Philip, immigrated to America in 1909. Philip knew how to write, so he reported to the family the joyous sight of seeing the Statue of Liberty from the deck of his steamer. From Ellis Island he traveled to Chicago, hoping to make enough money to send for his wife and fourteen children.

Motivated by Philip's accounts of his new life, William and Santa came to America in 1910. Although an experienced barber, William was unable to pass the barber's certification because he could not speak English. For several years he worked for a railroad in Indiana but eventually obtained his barber's license. William made his home on Taylor Street in Chicago, an area known as "Little Italy."

Initially my ancestors were enthralled with America. Having subsisted from day to day on meager portions of olives, fish, bread and pasta in Sicily, they were overwhelmed by how people could store food in their homes in cupboards and pantries and the newest item of modern technology—the icebox. To them it was like having a store in your own home.

They had expected to work hard, and they did, often in sweatshops. They were often exploited, although they did not rebel. The women also took in sewing, working by gaslight late into the evening.

The Italians soon learned that they were the lower class. The Irish, who had settled in large American cities earlier, had gained both political and economic power. To the Germans, Irish and English, the Sicilians were illiterate, overemotional and worthy objects of discrimination. It is not surprising that with the courts and the police dominated by Irish and Germans, the Mafia would grow in the Italian ghettos. Initially they were looked on with favor, even by my grandparents in Chicago.

As the Chicago Italians banded together for mutual support, they created a Little Italy in which they could maintain their culture, customary diet, traditions and language. By 1916, there were almost 200,000 Italians in Chicago living near Taylor Street and Blue Island. The cobblestone streets were lined with peddlers selling fruit, vegetables and fresh fish from behind box stands. Mixed in with the clatter of streetcars and horse-drawn carts was the distinctive Sicilian dialect. Clothes were hung from lines between buildings and draped out of windows, and everywhere there were the sounds and sights of scurrying children.

My mother, Rose, was born that year in Chicago's Little Italy. Rose was the first child, sensitive and in many ways as fragile as the flower she was named for. Her mother was a strict disciplinarian but had a kind and generous heart. Her father doted on her, constantly buying her new clothes and giving large parties in her honor. In her sheltered and protected world, which only extended several blocks, everyone was a relative or a *paisan.*

The promise of the good life had come true for my mother's family. My grandfather William had his own barbershop with an impressive striped pole, motorized no less. His apartment was elaborately furnished. He also had one of the first radios, not a crystal set like most, but a wonderful-sounding radio in a large wooden cabinet. William was the first person on his block to own a car; in 1920 he bought a Chandler. His wife, Santa, who had owned only three simple print dresses in Marsala, now had many outfits, coordinated with matching hats, gloves, purses and shoes. My grandfather and his brothers were always impeccably dressed, with starched collars, ties, vests and patent-leather shoes.

William and Santa shared their prosperity with others. Their home was constantly open to friends and family, with food and wine in abundance. From the time my mother was four years old, she remembered the family gathering in their home on Sunday mornings for a large breakfast. All the food was fresh, and there were home-baked pastries, including Rose's favorite lemon-cream pie.

In 1922, my grandfather moved his family to Austin Avenue, and most of the relatives followed, living within several blocks. He bought a large apartment building, his family on the first floor, grandparents above, and aunt and uncle below.

The church was important to the family, but St. John Bosco, an Italian church on Austin Avenue, would not be erected until 1936. The closest Roman Catholic church was St. William's, but it was a Polish-speaking church. For this reason, everyone traveled back to the old neighborhood to Guardian Angel's Church on Forquer Street. There, Father Tony Coga preached in Italian. It was a long, but infrequent, trip. No one in my family attended church except for weddings, funerals and baptisms.

When my mother was six years old, she went away with her mother for the weekend. When she returned, she smelled a strong odor coming from the door leading to the basement. She opened the door and saw a strange metal contraption. William immediately instructed his daughter not to venture into the basement while the still was there; he knew that stills could explode.

It wasn't his idea to have a still there, even though it only stayed several weeks. It was the Mafia already filtering into the people's basements. William had no choice. Some of his old-country friends, including the Genna brothers, had created their own power structure through crime. Angelo Genna had become a millionaire by working for mobster Al Capone, supplying him with illegal alcohol. The six Genna brothers had a large distillery on Taylor Street but spread out into Italian homes because the demand for bootleg whiskey was growing. They were the chief suppliers of Al Capone in Chicago and Johnny Torrio in New York.

The Mafia code from Sicily was now dominant in the Little Italy of Chicago and New York's Little Italy: never betray family, never talk to the police about illegal activities, and never mix family life with business. It was not difficult to understand how the Genna brothers acquired such overnight wealth, considering they produced the whiskey for forty cents a gallon and sold it for six dollars a gallon. Their use of violence kept competition away.

My mother knew the Genna brothers as family friends, but never knew that Angelo had a nickname, "Bloody Angelo." He would boldly walk down a street holding a pistol or a shotgun in open view. He paid as much as $200,000 a year to have the police ignore him. Sicilians like my grandfather probably feared him more than they respected him. Every Italian in Little Italy knew that Angelo had walked up to a man in broad daylight and shot him repeatedly in the head. Angelo had walked away from the scene slowly. Of course, there were witnesses, but no one ever came forward to testify.

The Genna brothers had another side to their natures. They gave my mother, Rose, money gifts at her first communion and at birthdays. They were generous and kind. They would sit around my grandparents' table eating pasta and sharing conversation with barbers, bricklayers and seamstresses. After dinner they would laugh, listening to humorous stories from the old country while eating fruit, nuts and rich Sicilian pastries.

For Rose's ninth birthday party over thirty relatives and friends crowded into the basement. Two long tables—actually plywood planks on sawhorses—were draped with white tablecloths. As usual for a party, the meal lasted for three or four hours, with long breaks between courses for conversation, the smoking of a fine cigar or even an occasional nap. After the dinner, the smell of garlic still lingered in the air. The group had feasted on zucchini topped with mozzarella cheese, eggplants deep fried in olive oil with garlic and parsley, huge bowls of spaghetti with a rich meat sauce the Italians called gravy, and ample Marsala wine and Italian bread. This was followed by a large salad with oil-and-vinegar dressing. It was an Italian custom to eat the salad after the meal, not as the Americans do at the beginning.

Now as several family musicians played folk songs from the old country, two heavy women came down the basement stairs from the kitchen with platters of Sicilian pastry, including cannoli (a fried pastry filled with ricotta cheese and flavored with wine, candied fruit and powdered sugar). Rose was served first as it was her birthday.

As Rose selected a pastry she turned to see a gentleman come down the stairs. It was Angelo Genna. He had a broad smile, dark penetrating eyes and slick, black hair. His physical appearance was striking. He was wearing a broad-brimmed fedora hat, a cashmere coat, gloves and white spats. As usual, there was a fresh carnation on his jacket lapel. To a young girl he was a prince charming.

Rose was surprised that the man commanded so much respect from her father. William quickly got up and offered Genna his chair near the head of the table. Her father always appeared to be a strong and decisive man in the family. He had no difficulty summoning commands or giving steely eyed glances that signaled disapproval to the children. But Rose could not understand why her father looked meek, even fearful of their prominent guest. He was so eager to please. Only she noticed that her father's hand shook as he eagerly poured wine into the guest's glass.

Outside their apartment building was Genna's large black Lincoln. Two bodyguards stood at the front entrance, one stood at the rear, and an armed driver sat in the car. Angelo and his brothers usually came in the dark of night, so Rose rarely saw the bodyguards stationed outside.

On Sundays Angelo or one of his five brothers would come to the door of each fellow Sicilian for the collection. The money would be used to get a friend out of jail, or raise enough money to bring relatives to America. Rose's father always gave money to the collection. My grandfather never contemplated, not for a moment, declining their gentle request. There was whispered talk of injuries, house burnings or bombings. After the collection, Rose's father and mother would talk behind closed doors in animated, loud conversation. Rose always wondered what they were talking about.

Though Angelo seemed to have every base covered, soon after his marriage to the daughter of a respected Italian politician, Henry Spignola, his protection ran out. As he drove down Ogden Avenue, a large sedan containing Frank Gusenberg (Bugs Moran's bodyguard) and Earl "Hymie" Weiss (paid killer for Moran) drove alongside him. They opened fire, and Bloody Angelo was killed. Angelo had hired Al Capone's hit men, Scalise and Anselmi, to kill a prominent Irish mobster, Dion O'bannion. This act was meant to avenge O'bannion's death.

The headlines read: "Mobster Slain in Gang War." But as a child, my mother, Rose, only remembered a dignified man eating in her home. For my grandparents and other relatives, the news of deaths was accepted. They were the casualties of war, after all. Sicilians were fighting to keep their honor and territory.

My grandparents sat in the church during the gangster's funeral. Life-size statues of saints and plaster angels gazed down from alcoves. The Sicilians believed in funerals as large as weddings. With 3,000 guests, Angelo's wedding had been the largest wedding Chicago had ever seen; now his funeral six months later was the largest funeral in Chicago's history, with a solid bronze casket, thousands of people lining the streets and twenty flower cars filled with flowers to be spread around Angelo's grave at Mt. Carmel Cemetery. Rose counted them as they drove past.

The infighting in this Italian community continued. And the bloody mess certainly shaped my grandparents' and parents' view of the world. Not long afterward, the same two hit men, Scalise and Anselmi, went after Angelo's brother Mike. They got him in their car, intending to kill him, but police pulled alongside the car, and a gun battle broke out. Several police officers were killed. One policeman shot Mike Genna in the leg, and Mike bled to death after a purposely slow ambulance ride. Scalise and Anselmi escaped.

Then the violence touched our family. Rose's uncle Vito Cappitelli was returning to his boarding house. A man approached him and greeted him with a handshake. The man held tightly to his hand as another man ran up from behind and shot Vito in the back of the head. Rose was told it was a case of mistaken identity.

My grandfather was careful to remain passive toward gang activity. Mobsters would come into my grandfather's barbershop on Cicero near Harrison. They talked about sports and music and the old country, but William was smart enough never to talk about their "business."

What was it like to be a woman among all this? My mother, Rose, learned that to be an Italian woman was to be a hard worker

who did not ask too many questions. She was not to ask why
Uncle Vito was killed, or what some of their friends did for a
living. Italian women cleaned the house, took care of the children, slept with their husbands and did not talk about business.
They never asked where the money came from. The important
thing was that a man was a good provider, was tender and affec-
tionate with the children, and went to church on the holy days
of obligation. A good Sicilian wife in Little Italy made sure that
food was on the table when her husband came home, that his
shirts were laundered and ironed when he needed them. If a
stranger came to the house to discuss business with her husband,
she would bring in food and drink, close the door and leave them
alone.

In 1926 Rose celebrated her first communion. She was dressed
like a bride in a beautiful white lace dress with a matching white
veil. She marched up the aisle, hands pressed together like an
angel, and received the body of Christ. At the communion party,
a tall, thin man with dark eyes and dark hair, John Scalise, was
kind to her. A few years later, John Scalise came to her home for
her cousin's engagement party. Rose danced with him and
thought, "What a fine gentleman!"

Some feared Scalise had the evil eye, as one of his eyes was
out of alignment. Superstition aside, he was among the worst
men in Chicago. He was wanted for murder in Sicily, and the year
before Rose's first communion he had killed Tony and Mike
Genna before becoming a hit man for Al Capone. Scalise would
dip his bullets in garlic, believing it would cause an infection if
his shots were not deadly accurate.

On January 20, 1929, Rose's thirteenth birthday, her parents
gave her still another festive party. Another family friend from
Marsala, Albert Anselmi, asked Rose to dance with him. She
thought of him as an old man, partly because he was balding,
portly and short. To a girl of thirteen, a man in his early thirties
can seem much older. As they danced she was charmed by his
good graces and manners. Rose never suspected that he was
wearing two, possibly three guns—or that some of the visitors to

her house were among the most deadly and feared men in Chicago.

Several weeks after Rose's birthday party, on St. Valentine's Day, Anselmi joined his partner, John Scalise, and several other Capone hit men. They put on police uniforms and rode in a large, black sedan down Clark Street. They arrived at a garage which was the headquarters for Bugs Moran. Inside the garage they lined up seven members of the Moran gang and killed them in a spray of machine-gun fire. Another time of revenge had come. No one was ever brought to trial for the St. Valentine's Day massacre.

With their growing power came growing mistrust of each other. Angelo Genna had once contracted Scalise and Anselmi to kill Al Capone. They were vicious, but they weren't crazy. They worked as double agents for years—working for Genna, yet keeping Capone informed. After Angelo Genna's death in 1925, they became the personal bodyguards for Al Capone. Yet, Capone never forgave Anselmi and Scalise for even entertaining the Genna proposition to kill him. Eventually the crooked-eyed Scalise and the round-faced Anselmi were given several moments to pray as they knelt before Capone who himself ended their lives with a baseball bat.

Frequently on Sunday afternoons my grandfather William would take his family for a long ride to Mt. Carmel Cemetery. There they would spend several hours seated on folding chairs and having a picnic lunch at the graveside of Rose's great-grandmother, Rose Casano, her grandfather, Vincenzo Titone, Uncle Vito and others. The family called it "visiting the dead." It wasn't a morbid activity but a time to remember loved ones.

Later in the afternoon, Rose and her mother would walk down the roadway, arms locked, looking at the large stone mausoleums with family names etched above the doorways. Each mausoleum contained room for six coffins and often had a small altar, a stained-glass window and a statue.

Rose would peer through the glass of the locked metal doors, in some cases remembering people who had been in her home. She peered into the Genna tomb which contained the bodies of

Angelo Genna, killed in 1925 by the Moran gang; Mike and Tony Genna, killed separately in 1925 by Scalise and Anselmi on orders of Capone; and later to be joined by Jim Genna's body, when after returning from Marsala, surgeons would be paid off to end his life during a routine operation. In 1947 at the age of forty-eight, Capone's body would be put in a grave yards from the Genna crypt.

Family secrets were an important Sicilian value. No one talked about crime or the bad side of a friend or relative. In some ways dishonesty was praised, and Rose developed her value system by listening to these discussions.

For instance, one family conversation concerned my grandfather's oldest brother, Philip Cappitelli, a postman. In 1930 when Rose was fourteen years old, she had heard that Philip had found an unattended briefcase which contained $80,000 in government bonds. He turned it over to the police, and he received a reward of $150, with which he bought a new suit. His name also appeared in the newspaper. But some family members considered him too honest—even stupid. Years later my mother would tell me that she thought Uncle Philip was foolish not to have kept the money.

Perhaps the most important thing Rose learned from her family was loyalty, and a distrust of strangers. Strangers were anyone non-Italian and non-family. This included newspaper reporters, police and virtually anyone who criticized the family. She was aware of the violence of Little Italy, but it was only murder or crime when committed by a non-Italian. Italians shot in self-defense and did things to help their families. With all the turmoil, Rose's world view remained simplistic. At her sixteenth birthday party, surrounded by relatives and friends, gangland wars seemed unimportant.

Perhaps because she was overprotected, Rose developed many fears—fears of everything from animals to lightning and elevators. But she never feared the gangsters who came into her home. They were, after all, family. No one who provided for a wife, loved his children and ate at the same table with you should be feared, she reasoned.

So Rose remembered the parties and special occasions, the singing and dancing—not the danger that haunted the streets. This was the old neighborhood of the old days that my mother talked about so much as I grew up. I always felt sad for her. She talked about those days so longingly, as if they were never to be recaptured, as if the best of times was in the past.

* * *

At the same time my mother was being raised in Chicago's Little Italy, my father was growing up in the Little Italy of Brooklyn, New York. He was my mother's cousin Matthew, born in Marsala in 1911. Before Matthew's birth, his father, Vincenzo Smorto, had come to America to settle in Brooklyn. Vincenzo's wife, Carmella, joined him with Matthew and their other children two years later.

My grandmother Carmella was a brave woman. She had endured her sister Theresa's unjust arrest for murder and that beloved sister's exile and death. But even Carmella was confused by the large crowd and turmoil of Ellis Island. She held two-year-old Matthew's hand firmly. At the end of the processing, she disembarked from the ferry at the New York City docks and joined her husband, who had never seen his son.

Once the family was reunited, more children were born. Once the family was complete, Matthew was the middle child of three brothers and three sisters. The children had strong relationships. His two older sisters mothered, protected and spoiled him, but his whole life was not centered around home.

When my parents traveled back to my father's neighborhood in Brooklyn many summers during my growing-up years, I came to know the streets, the stores, the flats and the brownstones that my father had known as a child. It was obvious that Matthew was very much a boy at home on the streets.

Matthew attended Brooklyn's PS38 and was soon known as Marty by his school friends. He was a curious, independent boy who freely roamed the streets with his pals. They pitched pennies, stole apples from carts and generally carried out mischief.

By age ten he was fascinated with horses, and wearing knickers, high socks, high brown shoes, white shirt and white sailor hat, he would take ten-cent rides in a local park. In the only photograph I've ever seen of my father as a young boy, he is perched on a horse.

Marty looked like a young Clark Gable and kept himself in good physical shape, working out at the local gym. There he would watch up-and-coming boxers sparring. Marty dropped out of school in the eighth grade and turned to amateur boxing, earning the Golden Glove award and then turning professional. When he wasn't fighting, he was attending boxing matches. His robust, ex-merchant-marine father approved of his son's activities, but his mother, Carmella, and his older sisters wanted to cultivate his more sensitive side. Each day he was made to practice the violin and take lessons, even when he reached his late teens. Here was a professional fighter who continued to practice the violin for his mother's approval!

My father was surrounded by the same casual violence my mother saw in Chicago. He knew Brooklyn to be a rough place, with Italian terrorists belonging to the Black Hand, the secret brotherhood that extorted money from other Italians for "protection." The Mafia closely linked Brooklyn and Chicago. Chicago gangster Al Capone was a Brooklyn native. He and another Italian gangster, Johnny Torrio, ran the prostitution houses in Brooklyn and other parts of New York. When my father was sixteen he observed a long funeral procession winding through Brooklyn. Franky Yale, a friend of Capone's who had helped in the Chicago murder of Dion O'bannion, had been killed himself at Capone's orders. The funeral procession was the largest Brooklyn had ever seen.

Concerned over the violence she saw everywhere, my grandmother Carmella wanted to keep Marty out of trouble. She was glad that Marty liked to dress like a gentleman and had friends that did the same. (At seventeen, Marty would frequent Prospect Park on weekends, dressed in a fine suit with matching vest and a straw hat.) Carmella didn't know Marty and his well-dressed friends spent some of their time drinking and gambling.

Actually, Marty had been gambling for years. From the time he was fourteen he had worked in a shoe-repair shop where he held back claim tickets, using the pocketed cash to gamble with. He spent most of his money with bookies on horse races. By age twenty, gambling was his preoccupation. His father, Vincenzo, who hadn't worked since he came to New York, collected money from all the children. Marty even held back money from him to use for gambling.

In 1932, after a two-year stint in the National Guard, Marty began to work as a longshoreman on the Brooklyn docks. He was twenty-two. It was tough, hard work, and the unions extorted large fees if the men wanted work. Marty was an independent young man. He had a small circle of Sicilian friends, an overprotective mother, overprotective sisters, an emotionally distant father and a gambling obsession.

The next year he visited Chicago and met my mother, Rose.

My parents, Rose and Marty, were both shaped by these larger-than-life rough and vicious times. This is the background they both took into marriage and parenthood, the background that shaped me. Yet their abrupt courtship, forced wedding and even more difficult relationship still reads as if someone made it all up.

Chapter 2

PARENTS

I T WAS THE SUMMER OF 1933 IN CHICAGO, AND ROSE, AT SEVEN-
teen, had just graduated from Austin High School. At his
barbershop, my grandfather William proudly boasted about
his daughter's talent. She was one of the first family members to receive a diploma and was now earning money by giving
piano lessons at her home and playing at the local community
center at Reese Park.

That summer, as before, the New York relatives came to visit.
My grandfather's first cousin Carmella Smorto brought her son
Marty, whom Rose had not seen in several years while he was in
the military and working.

At first sight, Rose thought Marty looked like Clark Gable, with
his large brown eyes, slick black hair and impeccable appearance.
At the same meeting, Marty decided Rose was beautiful—her eyes
were blue, her hair was curly, and her figure was worthy of a
model. They began to fall in love, but they told no one. In traditional Italian families at that time, parents matched couples. In
rare instances where no match was made, a man needed permission from the woman's father. No one thought of matching Marty
and Rose because they were second cousins.

By now, Marty was playing the violin so well that he was taking lessons from the concert master of the New York Philharmonic. He and Rose played together at family parties and gatherings. Aside from what she saw on this visit and their common appreciation for music, Rose knew very little of Marty's day-to-day life in New York. She believed he was respectful and gentle. Marty the boxer, the gambler and the hot-tempered Sicilian were all strangers to her.

In secret, Marty and Rose shared their love for one another. When they walked together, there were no chaperones, since no one knew of their intentions. By the end of the summer, Rose was dreaming of her storybook wedding, perhaps in one or two years. One evening, Marty asked her to marry him—immediately. Rose refused. That was impossible! There were too many details to arrange first: bridesmaids, dresses, reception hall. Upset by her resistance, Marty left her home abruptly.

The next day, Rose was giving a piano lesson in her parlor when she heard voices shouting and dishes crashing in the kitchen. Marty had come in the back door drunk. As Rose's parents and uncle tried to subdue him, Rose rushed to the kitchen.

She was frightened by the sight of a stranger—Marty as a wild man! His usually groomed appearance was gone; his clothes were disheveled and his hair unruly. He was weaving and stumbling into furniture. Marty, of course, was a professional fighter, and holding him was almost impossible. More relatives entered the kitchen to help, grabbing his arms and then his legs. Suddenly, in his stupor, Marty blurted out that he and Rose were engaged. Rose was shocked, as were her parents.

"Is this true?" William said, turning to his daughter.

Rose lowered her eyes to the floor and sheepishly said, "Yes."

My grandmother gasped, putting her hands to her mouth. Why this terrible break with tradition? How could this romance have blossomed under their eyes?

After Marty calmed down, he slept the night. The next morning, tired and embarrassed, he was promptly put on a train back to Brooklyn. Rose's and Marty's parents talked by phone. When all the blaming was put aside, the parents decided to make the best of the situation. They would allow the courtship to continue by phone and by mail while plans would be made for a proper wedding. From then on, next to her piano playing and lessons, Rose spent most of her time planning the wedding. Although there had been no elaborate engagement party, every detail of this church wedding would meet with the standards of tradition.

The following spring, Marty returned to Chicago to live at his friend Sammy's house. Now whenever Marty and Rose met, there were older Italian ladies, often widows, as chaperones. If they went for a walk, the chaperones were a few feet behind. If they were sitting in the parlor, the chaperones were sitting in the same room.

One particular evening, Marty picked up Rose to take her to see a movie. It was six o'clock when he drove up in Sammy's car. She was surprised to find Sammy beside him. Marty and Sammy were good friends, but Rose didn't like him. She had heard rumors from her parents that Sammy worked for the Mafia, collecting bets from bookies.

Rose encouraged her younger brother Frank to come along for the ride. But when the men stopped off for some beers, Frank stayed behind (Marty had given him some money so he would take the streetcar home). When Marty, Rose and Sammy continued on alone, instead of going directly to the movie theater, they headed for a neighborhood Rose did not recognize.

Slowly Marty circled the same block twice. He parked in a dark area and fumbled under the seat. By the lights of a passing car, Rose saw him pull out a large, black gun. He checked the revolver to see that each chamber had a bullet.

"What's that for?" she said nervously.

"I've got to catch a guy that owes me some money," he responded.

Marty left the car, walked down the street and disappeared in the doorway of an apartment building. Rose was scared. She didn't talk to Sammy, who was still sitting in the back seat of the car, but she glanced over her shoulder and noticed that he too was holding a gun.

Soon Marty returned, walking briskly to the car. More to Sammy than to Rose, he said curtly, "Everything's fine."

At last, they were on their way, but now they pulled up to a house on Taylor Street. As they did, Marty turned to Rose and said, "Get down on the floor."

Rose was too nervous to question. Huddled down on the floor, her heart pounding and her breathing labored, she thought she would faint. This time both Sammy and Marty got out of the car. It was getting late, which made her worry about what her parents might think. Soon the door opened, and Marty and Sammy got in the front seat with Rose still crouched on the floor between them.

"It's okay now," Marty told her. "You can get up."

"Marty," Rose said, "I want to go home."

Marty assured her that everything was okay, that he had gotten the money owed him.

Now there was a third stop, Sammy's home. Rose was bewildered. Sammy left, but in a few minutes returned holding a small duffle bag he threw into the back seat. Sammy's mother leaned into the car, gave Rose a smile and then said to Marty, *"Buona fortuna, Matteo,"* which meant "Good luck, Marty."

Now sitting in the middle, with Sammy on her right and Marty driving, Rose kept quiet, but her mind was a whirl of questions. As they crossed a bridge near Calumet City, she knew they were moving away from her neighborhood. The air was humid, the sky dark and the scenery distinctively rural. They were in Indiana, and it was almost midnight. Marty announced that they were headed for Crown Point, Indiana, where they would find a justice of the peace and get married.

Rose was shocked. She had never once contemplated eloping. What would her parents think? What about her wedding plans? As much as she loved Marty, her overriding emotion was fear. Sammy and Marty both had guns. She was terrified by the enraged Marty she had seen the summer before.

At two o'clock in the morning, my grandfather was becoming more and more angry as he looked out the front window to the street below. My grandmother, wearing her bathrobe, was pacing in the kitchen. Then my grandfather caught a glimpse of the streetcar stopping at the Austin and Grand intersection. His son, Frank, emerged, clearly alone.

In a moment of fury, William let out a yell. Santa came running into the living room. He knew what had happened: his daughter had eloped. He assumed Rose was a willing part of the plot.

"Where is Rosa?" William yelled at Frank, grabbing him by his coat lapels.

Frank did not know. Santa pleaded with William to calm down, but he stormed out the front door and ripped the sign for piano lessons off the front of the building and threw it into the street. Then he disappeared into the cellar, only to emerge with a hatchet in order to break up the piano in the parlor. His wife and children did all they could to hold him back. Other relatives awakened and came to help calm him down.

At the same time, Marty was waking up a justice of the peace. The wedding ceremony lasted only ten minutes. When the justice of the peace wanted to make sure Rose was of legal age, Sammy increased his usual fee. In moments the documents were signed.

Meanwhile on Austin Avenue, my grandfather seemed to be calming down. Rose's mother was thinking of the shame of an elopement in the family, but she knew she would be able to forgive Rose and Marty when they returned in a few days.

However, it was soon clear that William's calmness was based on a determination to act, not to forgive. He told Santa he was going for a ride. She was terrified. Before he and one of his brothers left in his car, William loaded one of his shotguns and put a handful of 12-gauge shells in his coat pocket. William was an avid hunter of rabbits and quail, but now he was hunting for his new son-in-law. My grandfather made several stops, including Sammy's house, but no one gave him any information about the couple, which made him even more angry.

By now, Marty had driven back to Chicago to the South Shore Hotel and checked in under a false name. Marty and Rose spent their four-day honeymoon in their hotel room. Sammy brought in meals and usually camped outside the door, wearing his concealed gun. He was more than the best man, he was Marty's bodyguard during those four days. And a bodyguard was needed; Sammy and Marty both knew what a Sicilian temper was like, especially an enraged father's.

The first morning, Rose woke up hoping that she'd only had a nightmare, but she knew it was real when she saw Marty's revolver on the dresser. She had longed for the lovely church ceremony, the festive wedding party, the beautiful dress. Not having a church wedding is something my mother would regret the rest of her life.

At the end of the week, Marty informed Rose that he was taking her to New York. She was stunned. He said leaving town was necessary to give her father time to cool off. Rose thought she would be going away for several weeks, but Marty had no intention of bringing her back home. Rose had never traveled farther than Detroit; now she was headed for Brooklyn, and she had no idea that it would be almost ten years before she would return home.

Marty and Rose Smarto (Marty changed his name from *Smorto* to *Smarto* to avoid being confused with an uncle) began their married life in a grimy, little apartment on Market Street near the waterfront. Rose had never known poverty; her family had lived well in Chicago. Her father had provided whatever she needed or wanted. But from the time they got to Brooklyn, Marty was out of work, and Rose found herself on welfare. She had been accustomed to abundant food in the pantry, but now she used food stamps and waited in line with the other poor people. Rose spent most of her time crying and complaining that she missed home. As a result, Marty's older sisters and mother disliked her.

Since the families were related, the Smortos did not want the Cappitellis to know how their daughter was living. One day while Rose was writing a letter home, Carmella, Marty's mother, entered the kitchen and said, "What is she doing?"

Before Rose had a chance to say anything, Carmella lurched to the table and crumpled the letter that Rose was writing. "I don't want her writing to her family," Carmella said to Marty.

Not having heard from their daughter in months, the Cappitelli family notified the police. The Chicago police in turn contacted the New York police, who sent a policewoman looking for Rose. One day a policewoman came to Rose's apartment and asked her directly if she was being held against her will. Marty, his mother and sisters were in the room. Rose looked around at the solemn faces and told the policewoman, "No."

It was now the spring of 1935, and Rose was expecting her first child. Marty was working one or two days a week as a longshoreman on the docks. It was hard work and sporadic. He would spend the rest of the time with his friends, gambling in the back of a local bar or at the horse track.

Because they were poor, when it came time for Rose to deliver, she had to go to the county hospital as a charity patient. At the time of the delivery, Marty was at the racetrack, gambling away money his older sister had given him. Because of restricted visiting privileges, it was three days after the delivery before he saw his first child, my brother Joseph.

Soon Rose was back home with her baby boy, looking at the world from her hot tenement apartment. Occasionally there would be a religious procession in the street below, and she would catch a glimpse of her father-in-law, Vincenzo, pinning money to a statue of the Virgin Mary. Although Rose did not attend church, she kept to her religious practices faithfully and had many statues, including a favorite of the Madonna. Her belief in God comforted her during these depressing days.

Marty's gambling and irritability grew. One day he convinced Rose to go to the racetrack with him to see the famous horse Whirlaway. Rose only went because Marty convinced her that the hot dogs at the racetrack were among the finest. She watched him bet on each race, and she watched him lose on every bet. They returned by train from Long Island to Brooklyn, not having eaten all day because there was no money left for food.

Things got worse. When Marty lost at the track, he came home angry. One afternoon during a heated argument, Marty smashed

Rose's prized Madonna statue to the floor. He replaced it, but during a subsequent argument he took that statue too and smashed it.

Secretly, Rose was saving up for train fare to visit her family in Chicago. She finally had twenty-seven dollars, the price of a ticket. When she received word that her maternal grandmother Josephine had died, she looked into the jar and discovered the money missing. Marty had taken it and lost it gambling. Several months later, her paternal grandfather died, but again there was no money to attend the funeral.

As I grew up, I remember my mother comparing her days in Brooklyn to being a prisoner. She always insisted she loved my father but stayed with him more out of fear than tenderness.

In 1940, Rose became pregnant again. She remembered with hurt her experience in the county hospital, so decided to have her second child at home. But when she went into labor, the midwife couldn't be located. Only Marty was present, and he saved the life of his second child, who was born with the umbilical cord wrapped around his neck. The second boy was named Anthony.

Rose was now raising two boys and doing her best to make ends meet. But after the home birth, she was weak and feverish, and her immune system was so poor that she developed a serious leg infection. During these years, Rose had made one trip back to Chicago with her first son. Now her mother, Santa, made a trip to New York to care for her sick daughter. All too soon Santa returned to Chicago. Marty still spent most of his time with his doting mother and sisters, his small circle of friends and his gambling. Rose felt isolated and alone once more.

I never saw my father physically abuse my mother. Never hitting women was a restraint Marty learned from his mother and sisters. Even so, Rose knew Marty was capable of great violence and destruction; his quickness to smash things when angry was only one indication. One day Rose learned that Marty had beaten a man on the street who owed him money from a gambling debt. The word on the street was that if people had not come to the man's assistance, Marty may well have killed the man. Rose lived in fear that that powerful anger would be unleashed on her or their children.

Although Marty was no longer boxing professionally, he kept telling Rose that he wanted his oldest son to be a boxer. One of the first gifts Marty gave to Joseph was a miniature pair of boxing gloves. However, my mother didn't want her children to learn to be violent. Weekly my parents had fierce arguments over how to raise the kids.

Rose's in-laws did not visit often; Rose and Marty's apartment was too small for much company. However, one day when the family was coming, Rose was making every effort to have everything just right. While she was cooking, a cab driver brought Marty home drunk. Marty's sisters and brother arrived soon after and put Marty to bed after a long struggle. When Vincent and Carmella arrived, they were simply told that their son was sick.

The tiny apartment was so hot that after dinner everyone brought chairs to the roof of the building. While the party was relaxing and sipping wine, Rose heard a loud and fiendish laugh. Marty was standing in the doorway that led to the roof. His silhouette was unmistakable in the light cast by a bare ceiling light behind him. Not until he began walking closer did she see the gun in his right hand.

She exclaimed, "Marty, put that gun down!"

His family said nothing. Only his younger brother Lou comforted Rose, "Don't worry. He's not going to hurt anyone."

Marty went to the edge of the roof and began to fire the gun into the air. *Bang! Bang! Bang!* The sound echoed down the street. Marty wasn't angry or wild; he was just happy. *Bang! Bang! Bang!* Rose flinched with each shot. She hadn't known Marty still had a gun and wondered where he had kept it. She tried not to show it, but in the years to come she continued to live in fear.

As I was growing up, my mother would often tell me that something was wrong with my father's brain because he had been punched in the head too often. I wondered if that was true.

In 1943, Marty's mother died. Rose had never felt very close to her mother-in-law, who had been cruel to her in many ways. Carmella's funeral was a typical New York Italian funeral held at home, which my mother found morbid. Rose looked toward the open bedroom door, watching the funeral director put up a sheet. When a funeral was held at home, the embalming was done there as well. She could not ignore the sounds and smells of the embalmer's art.

When the embalmer finished, Carmella's body was put in a satin-lined, metal coffin and placed in the parlor. The indirect torch lights cast a pallid glow in the room. There were flowers everywhere, including a large arrangement representing the face of a clock, with the hands indicating the exact time of death—another tradition. A rosary was intertwined in Carmella's fingers, a small crucifix placed against the open lid of the coffin and a large crucifix resting on a stand next to a red vigil light.

Many relatives pressed into the parlor, and with the heat of summer and the lack of air conditioning, the air in the room was stale. The women wore black, and like many Italian celebrations, the funeral lasted three days and three nights, with people taking turns keeping the vigil throughout. Rose had to take her turn after midnight on the second day and did so with her sister-in-law, Rose, who was married to Marty's oldest brother. The vigil was an obligation, and Rose couldn't help wishing she were anywhere else but there.

Carmella's daughters carried on in the mannerisms of the old country—crying, screaming, even swooning in a dead faint. At the cemetery, it was customary to open the lid of the coffin one last time. Emotions renewed. In the back of Rose's mind during the funeral, she was thinking of Carmella's death as the possibility for her getting back to Chicago.

In 1944, Rose did return home, after being gone nearly ten years. Perhaps because Rose was so determined not to stay in New York, she, Marty and the children moved back into her father's apartment building on Austin Avenue. My oldest brother, Joseph, was nearly ten, and my brother Anthony was four years old. Everything looked the same on Austin Avenue physically, and

Rose tried to convince herself that nothing had changed. But much *had* changed.

Rose's younger sister, Josephine, who had always stayed close to home and had been a devout churchgoer, belonging to the Sodality (a group that prayed faithfully to the Sacred Heart of Jesus), now had drifted away from the church. She was working as an usherette at the Chicago Opera House and was dating a divorced Russian Jew. In time, Josephine would marry this man whom she loved deeply, and in doing so renounce Christianity for all practical purposes.

Rose's younger brother, Frank, had lost his idealism and health while fighting in World War 2 in the South Pacific. The shock of the Guadalcanal battles and his recurring attacks of malaria left him shaken and irritable. At the time Rose returned to Chicago, Frank was married and had a young son, but his marriage was moving quickly toward divorce.

Rose wanted desperately for her relationship with her mother to continue from where it left off, but she knew the elopement and the years of separation had been particularly hard on Santa. There would be no time to renew the relationship, however. In that first year after Rose returned, her mother contracted pneumonia. Rose watched her slip away. One particular day, my grandmother's condition worsened. The doctor told Rose he wanted to speak to her father at once. She called him at the barbershop, but the other barber said he had left hours earlier. William was discovered sitting in a movie theater with another woman. Several days later, Rose's mother died.

The next year, in 1946, Marty's father died. Leaving my brothers with her sister Josephine, Rose and Marty returned to New York for the funeral. It was during this visit to Brooklyn that I was conceived. I was born back in Chicago.

Rose had just given birth to me, her third son, when a hospital nun said to my mother, "What do you want to name your boy?"

"Dominic," she replied, the name of an Italian saint.

The nun said gently, "You are in America now, Mrs. Smarto— the name is Donald."

Rose agreed.

A month later, I was brought to the baptistry of St. John Bosco Church, dressed in a long, handmade baptismal gown, and held by John and Concetta D'Amico, who from that day forward would be my godparents, an honor which meant that they were responsible for my religious education if something should happen to my parents.

Back at home there was a party. The priest who performed the baptism rite was seated at the head of the table, drinking wine and smoking a large cigar. My brothers, then eleven and six, were playing with wooden guns on a large sedan car beside the building. My mother remembered past festive celebrations in the basement; she deeply mourned the loss of her mother.

Several months after the baptism, my grandfather William announced he was moving to southern California. He had plans to buy a small farm. Rose was shocked. For years her father had begged her to return to Chicago. Now, with her mother dead, he was going to the other side of the world! Until his return to Chicago in the 1970s as a sick man, and his eventual death in 1977, my grandfather lived a very independent life, remarrying another four times, something about which the family never talked.

I was four years old when my parents bought a house in the suburbs, miles from the old neighborhood. In many ways, the move threatened my mother. However, the old neighborhood was no longer the same, either. The familiar families had spread out, some to other states. Gone forever was that certain sense of closeness, the spontaneous parties, the quick trips downstairs or across the street to talk to a relative.

Another thing my mother missed was the sense of identity with the local church. St. John Bosco, staffed by Italian priests, was only several feet from my mother's home on Austin Avenue. The new neighborhood in the suburbs was a mixture of Germans, Irish, Poles, Czechs and Italians, and our new church, more than three miles away, was equally a mixture.

Looking back on how God began to develop and nurture me,

I can see many signs of early grace. My two brothers had been raised in the Bronx. My oldest brother, especially, had seen family arguments and battles, but now that my mother was once again in Chicago, I truly was a peacetime baby. In America, it was an era of new prosperity, new jobs and housing. And my father settled down into a good job. At the time I was born, he worked for the United Shoeworkers Union, traveling primarily throughout the Midwest, negotiating union-dispute settlements. Though the unions were very tough and physical battles common, my father was very successful in settling disputes. He worked for the Union for about ten years before moving into a management position with Metropolitan Shoe Company, and later with Dr. Scholl's.

There were other positive changes in my family too. My older brothers both had a parochial education, and the teachers presented a stern picture of God. My parents decided to send me only to public schools. Perhaps this was a blessing, since my loving, nurturing mother was my sole source of religious instruction for the first twelve years of my life, and she painted a loving picture of God.

However the details of Christianity were not very clear in my mind. My mother talked to me often about the pope. He was, as she would say, "the closest thing to God on earth." When I was born, the reigning pope was Pius XII, born Eugenio Pacelli. I realize now that my mother's affection for the pope was not based strictly on church teaching but on the simple fact that he and his predecessors were Italian.

I did not attend church except at Easter and Christmas, when my brother Anthony would walk me, holding my hand. There was no Bible in our home. Somehow in my young, impressionable mind, Santa Claus, the Easter Bunny and God were merged together. Jesus was mentioned in the context of being Mary's son, but I didn't understand his relationship to God. Obviously, my understanding of God was faulty, but I did see God favorably— that God loved us and wanted to protect us, even as Mother Cabrini wanted to protect us.

A statue of Mother Cabrini was my favorite in our house. An

Italian immigrant who had settled in Chicago after the turn of the century, shortly after her death she became the first American to be declared a saint by the Catholic Church—a process that usually took at least a hundred years. July 7, 1946, the day of her cannonization, was a proud day for the Italian community. My mother kept St. Cabrini's statue under a glass dome which she constantly dusted. According to my mother, Mother Cabrini was a saint that someone in our family had personally met.

My grandfather William encountered St. Cabrini on Taylor Street one day as she picked up bricks from the site of a demolished building. According to my mother, the nun told William that she was saving the bricks to build a children's hospital. By all accounts, she was a woman of great vision, productivity and charity. Within the context of the turbulent gang wars of Little Italy, she was a shining light for the Italian community. My mother identified with this saint who knew the trials and struggles of the Italian immigrant in Chicago. Even at age five, I would look at the statue and believe that Mother Cabrini cared about our family.

Both in Sicily and in the Italian communities of New York and Chicago, religion was intertwined with family events and customs. Yet my family would be surprised about the part it would play in my life, and I would be surprised where it would carry me.

Chapter 3

CHILDHOOD

T HROUGHOUT MY CHILDHOOD, I HAD A HARD TIME GETTING A
clear picture of God. I once remember my mother sitting
me on her lap and telling me there was no Santa Claus.
She added that the Easter Bunny and the Tooth Fairy
didn't exist either. Even as a child of five I made a quick mental
leap to what seemed a logical conclusion. With quivering voice,
I asked, "Do you mean there is no God either?"

"Of course not," my mother said. "There is a God."

But it worried me. I'd always believed everything my mother
taught me, and now I wondered if she were simply holding this
last revelation for a better time.

Not attending parochial school, my religious education came
from my mother, who told me many religious stories. The stories
had nothing to do with the Bible; they were simply accounts of
saints' lives and miracles in recent centuries. In most of the stories where a saint or Mary appeared to people, they usually came
to a nun or priest, which gave me the impression that people in
holy orders were closer to God than laypeople. But the two stories I loved most and remember most vividly were about three
children in Fatima, Portugal, who saw the Virgin Mary, and about
a little girl in Lourdes, France, who saw the Virgin Mary and was

led to a spring of healing water. I preferred these stories because they were about people I could relate to.

I did not see nuns and priests very often, but when I did see a pair of nuns on the sidewalk, I knew they were saintly, because they were dressed just like the statue of Mother Cabrini back home. The priests too worked for the pope, and I looked at them with awe.

The summer I was nine years old my mother told me that the cardinal was coming to our church. I don't remember what the event was, but I remember the special impact of seeing him. My mother didn't drive, so hand in hand we walked the three miles to St. Gertrude's Church. The route took us behind several factory buildings and across several sets of railroad tracks to a place with little traffic.

Suddenly, my mother exclaimed, "There he is!"

I looked down the nearly empty street and saw a bright red car, like a fire chief's, and as it got closer, I saw a large gold cross on the door. It was Cardinal Stritch, the Archbishop of Chicago, a prince of the church. Immediately, my mother had us both on our knees. We were kneeling on the sidewalk as the car drove by, my mother making the sign of the cross to herself. The white-haired cardinal was busy talking and didn't even see us.

We sat in a pew near the back of the church. In the front, a throne had been erected for this special occasion. Suddenly, the procession began. The organ and choir were so loud I could feel the vibrations. Altar boys carrying candles and a crucifix led the procession, followed by many priests wearing white garments. Next, some forty Knights of Columbus, wearing red sashes and admiral hats with large plumes, marched up the aisle. They divided into two rows facing each other and then drew brightly polished silver swords which they raised and crossed.

The congregation was now standing and I stretched to get a glimpse of the cardinal. I saw his tall, pointed hat, called a miter, first. He was wearing bright silk robes with a long train carried by two pages. I was nervous as he passed. My mother knelt and made the sign of the cross again. Cardinal Stritch was the first

American to be a part of the Curia, the Vatican government, and he made frequent visits to confer with the pope. I remembered thinking that this man knows something that no one else does. He is closer to God than anyone else in this church. I longed to feel the presence of God in the way he did.

Holy Week was always a special time in my home. Between Palm Sunday and Easter Sunday we would refrain from eating meat. On Good Friday we fasted, and mom had a rule that the whole day we would not talk unless absolutely necessary. Also on Good Friday, as on Holy Saturday, we were not allowed to use the television, radio or record player. Around noontime my mother would look out the window and find a storm cloud that was to be her sign of the reenactment of the crucifixion weather.

At church during Lent the statues were covered with dark purple. As far as I ever knew, Holy Saturday, the day after Good Friday, was the one day of the year that my mother went to church. In our church, as in many, the statue of the crucified Christ was laid in the center aisle on a black catafalque. My mother felt she was attending a type of wake; being Italian, she put a great emphasis on wakes. She approached the statue of Christ slowly, as if it were a real body, and kissed the feet of the statue. Then I had to do the same.

During the short ceremony, in place of the usually bright agnus bells there was a wood clapper that made a loud, dull thud, as if to imitate the sounds of a nail being driven into a cross. It was a part of the liturgy I understood easily.

Growing up I believed the red vigil light next to the tabernacle signified the true presence of Jesus in the form of a communion wafer. The Saturday after Good Friday was the one day of the year when that light was extinguished. I remember how it disturbed me because it signified that the presence of God was gone. On that day, the sanctuary would seem cold and barren. I rarely thought of hell as a conflagration, but rather as an empty building—the loss of God's friendship.

The only other times I went to church were on the holy days, and holidays like Christmas and Easter. On the holidays, my mother was busy cooking and awaiting company, so my older brother Anthony would take me to church. He impressed me as having a strong faith, especially the day he told me, "I would put my arm in a fire for God."

The comment bewildered me. I couldn't imagine putting my arm in a fire for anything or anyone! I admired his faith and hoped that mine would be as strong some day.

We had a plastic jar containing holy water in our home. I refilled it from time to time at our church. Before going to bed each night, I would kneel in front of my bed and ceremonially spray the holy water on my bed in the shape of a cross. I always wore a scapular, a piece of cloth with the image of Mary on one side and Jesus on the other. Most every Italian relative I knew wore a chain with a religious medallion. At the same time they also wore something commonly called the "Italian horn," which I was taught could ward off evil.

In my bedroom in private, I would pretend to play mass. I would put a small missal on a dresser next to a small cup and imitate the gestures of the priests I had seen in church. My most frequent prayer was to have my parents stop fighting.

Without a Bible or any biblical pictures in my home, the only image I saw of Jesus was of a crucified body on a cross. The crucifix was in our home, and in almost every home we visited. Of all the statues and images I saw as a small child, one statue in particular left an indelible impression. Twice a month my parents and I would return to the old neighborhood on Austin Avenue and visit my godparents. While my father was in a smoke-filled back room playing cards and my mother sat in the parlor talking with the women, I would go to the entryway of their house, a quiet place sealed off by doors. There was one small light, a sconce that gave off a pinkish glow. The dim light was mounted on a wall near a statue of the head of the crucified Christ. It looked gory, with red paint used to depict the blood dripping from the crown of thorns and the wounds on the face.

I usually stayed a healthy distance from the sculpture. Wherever I stood, however, the eyes seemed to follow me. The face wasn't inviting or friendly, especially to a child. I never understood the blood on the face, and I never asked anyone why it was there. I knew that Jesus had died, and I knew he was a good person, but I couldn't understand his relationship with God. But the way the statue made me feel seemed to draw me to visit it again and again.

Once I was standing next to my mother on a street corner as she talked to a friend who had recently returned from Europe. My mother pointed out that around her friend's neck was a plastic amulet which contained a piece of the true cross on which Jesus had been crucified. From the moment of that declaration, I could not stop looking at the tiny sliver. I was thinking, *I wonder where the rest of the cross is. Who got the sliver off it? How was this lady lucky enough to get a piece?* I thought the piece of the cross had magical power and wished that I had one.

I hoped the annual visit from our priest would give our family some of that magical power. Once a year the priest would visit our home. I knew the event was important by the way my mother cleaned the house and my father put on a clean shirt. At the priest's expected time of arrival, the television was off, and we were fixed in our chairs, listening to the sound of the clock ticking. He was always punctual, and the sound of the doorbell made me jump slightly. I remember the tall figure of a man dressed in a large, black overcoat, wearing a large biretta, a black hat with a large black ball on it. He would hand his overcoat to my father, keep the biretta on his lap and be seated, dressed all in black except for the spot of white which was his Roman collar.

The conversation was casual, mostly about work and weather, rarely about spiritual matters, although the priest would always end with a phrase like, "I hope to see you in church Sunday." He didn't press the matter, and my parents never promised anything. The highlight of the thirty-minute visit was the priest's blessing of the house and us. We all would kneel, including my father, and the priest, using a small container of holy water, would spray water while making a large sign of the cross, intoning his blessing in Latin.

There was a lot about my home life the priest never got a glimpse of during his short visits. He was unaware of the frequent, almost daily, arguments between my parents, which usually centered around my father's gambling. He never knew that on our frequent trips to my godparents' home, my father and godfather always waited for the phone to ring at a certain time to receive a tip about a fixed raced from someone who worked at the racetrack. Though mostly these tips didn't pay off, sometimes they would win thousands of dollars this way.

My father's gambling certainly brought little prosperity and no joy to our home. Every Saturday evening my mother would be waiting for my father to come home from the track. I remember watching my mother peer through the Venetian blinds in the kitchen window, looking for his car. I could pick up her tension as she waited to discover the mood he would be in. If he had won, he would be happy. If he had lost, he would be angry.

One time I remember seeing my father enter and throw a fistful of ten-dollar and twenty-dollar bills in the air, which meant my mother should buy a new dress and we were going to eat at a restaurant. Those times were painfully few.

The more frequent times, when he lost, my mother would begin interrogating him. "How much did you lose, Marty?"

The arguing would begin. He would tell her it was none of her business, and she would tell him he was irresponsible. The screaming and yelling would last for hours, and eventually trail off into a kind of cold war, with no talk, just the sounds of slamming doors, cabinets and plates.

During the Saturday vigil anticipating my father's return from the racetrack, my mother would frequently share with me tales of how bad a husband or father he was. I would side with her and resent him. She told me how he lost three hundred dollars one night playing cards at a local tavern with friends, while only giving her ten dollars a week to feed three children. She also related how he had pawned her wristwatch, telling her he was taking it to a jeweler to have it fixed. He promptly lost the hundred dollars of pawn money on a horse race, and she never got the watch back. She recounted how almost every present given to her during her Brooklyn years disappeared into pawn shops, including her wedding ring. Fortunately, at least this one thing she got back.

In some ways, I tried to replace my father in her life. I tried to bring her some joy and comfort. I began feeling very angry toward him, although I could never express it. I saw little of my father, except on his terms.

My father had several racetracks he went to, depending on the season. On several occasions, he brought me with him, but I didn't enjoy those times. I always felt invisible to him. During a race he would stand near the finish line. It would frighten me to watch him screaming at his horse, veins bulging out on his forehead, his face bright red. If his horse lost, he would curse, turn pale and sullen, and then return to his racing form to study the next race.

Watching nine races with the long intervals in between made a terribly long and boring day for a child. I kept myself busy by walking through the stands and collecting the brightly colored used tickets. I would borrow my father's binoculars and look at other people in the stands. He never knew it, but sometimes from a distance I would watch him through the binoculars. He was always chainsmoking and intently studying the racing form. If at day's end he won, he would give me several dollars, but if he lost, there would be no talking in the car on the way home.

There was one day out of the year that I really looked forward to. Rain or shine, Dad would take me to the Brookfield Zoo. It would be just the two of us, together for the whole day. He would buy me hot dogs, popcorn and peanuts, and let me choose whatever animals I wanted to see in whatever order I preferred. That one day out of the year was most important because my father was doing something for me and me alone. Not surprisingly, even today I look back at those days at the zoo with great warmth.

The part of my father's Sicilian personality and temperament that saddened me the most was his ability to hold longstanding grudges. He would have fierce arguments with relatives that I loved; then they were put on his blacklist, meaning my mother, my brothers and I could not see or talk to them. Three such injustices seemed worse than the others. My father had banned us from communicating with my mother's sister, my Aunt Josephine. My mother and I would take two buses to visit her in a second-floor apartment in Chicago. One day my father showed up, and I remember everyone screaming at each other on the stairway.

Another time my father blacklisted my Uncle Frank, who was living with us after his marriage broke up. One day my father kicked him out and told us we could never see or talk to him again. I remember running into the back yard, crying. With no point of comparison, I assumed all families were like mine. I asked God why such things happened.

Though there were other relatives blacklisted from time to time, the final straw came when my godparents, who were very important to me, were put on his blacklist. My mother and I would sneak over to see them on Saturdays while my father was at the racetrack. I never liked feeling as if we were doing something wrong, even dangerous, behind my father's back.

Even my oldest brother, Joseph, was not immune from Dad's anger. Joe had acquired some of his father's habits. He would hang around a local bowling alley until early in the morning, often gambling. My father found out that Joe had stolen some cash that my father kept in a wooden cabinet in his bedroom. I was present when the argument erupted between my father and Joe. Joseph denied the theft. Dad essentially gave him an ultimatum: enlist in the Navy or else. My brother enlisted. That wasn't the end of the trouble, however. When Joseph was on a destroyer in the South Pacific, he started gambling on the ship, and my mother was constantly wiring him money. That caused fresh arguments between my father and mother. This, as had other facts, became a family secret. Though my father yelled fiercely about my oldest brother's gambling and theft, he and the whole family painted the best face on his enlisting in the Navy. Years later my mother would forget the circumstances entirely.

This was part of the dysfunction and pathology that made growing up in my family so difficult. I couldn't talk to a school counselor about the problems at home because one of the cardinal sins was talking about your family. I couldn't tell anybody I was scared or depressed. I simply had to keep things to myself. In many ways this drove me to God; I learned I could share more and more with him that I couldn't tell anyone else.

The older I got, communication seemed to be getting worse, not better, between my parents. I was ten when my mother and two other relatives decided to take a train trip to California to visit my grandfather. He had left the old neighborhood soon after I was born, and after a series of marriages and divorces was living on a little farm. I rarely knew the true reasons for most of my parents' arguments, but as we were about to enter the cab to the train station, my father came out of the house yelling and threw all our suitcases on the lawn. I remember my mother crying on the Union Pacific train most of the way to Los Angeles, and how frightened I felt about returning home!

We came home from California, and in his own way, my father tried to make up for our terrible sendoff by putting in the covered patio that my mother had long asked for. Her first reaction was, "What have you done? It's all wrong."

The responses by now were predictable. If she would ask him to do a household chore or repair, he would refuse out of stubbornness. When he got around to making the repair, she would say, "You never do anything right!"

By the time I was in junior high, anything could trigger an argument. I found holidays particularly stressful. Mingled with Thanksgiving, Christmas and Easter were stormy arguments, yelling and crying, with my father storming out of the room or out of the house. I can see now how both my parents were equally to blame, although as a child I thought it was always my father's fault. My mother would tell him he was cooking the turkey wrong, putting the Christmas tree up crooked or putting the wrong plates on the table. In particular, she would remind him of his faults in front of company. He would end up slamming something and walking off. Then she'd repeat her famous line, "He always ruins my holidays."

Years later, I would read Jean-Paul Sartre's "No Exit." That's exactly how living at home felt as a child. It was like a play that kept repeating itself. Each of my parents would talk in absolutes about the other. "You always do something," or "You never do something," they would say to each other.

It was probably part of their Italian upbringing, but they rarely showed affection in public. They didn't hold hands or kiss, or at least not when I was around. I have no recollection of affection between my parents. But if a friend or relative brought up the word *divorce* to my mother, she said that getting a divorce was out of the question. She often told me that she stayed in the marriage for the sake of her children.

The most frightening incident happened when I was seven years old, and it colored my perceptions from then on. My father came home from work without the raise he had expected. In fact, he felt his employer was cheating him. He was yelling and raving as he walked through the door. He picked up a heavy glass ashtray and smashed it into the wall, leaving a dent. He knocked over a chair and hit walls. I was so frightened that I was shivering.

The more my mother tried to calm him, the angrier he got. Suddenly, he went into a utility room off the kitchen and fumbled with the top over one of the double sinks. My mother was the first to hear the sound of a small, metal box opening. Then my father entered the living room with a black revolver.

"Marty!" my mother screamed. "Are you crazy? Put that away!"

He started waving the gun, and I feared that he would shoot all of us. My mother grabbed me by the hand, and together we ran out the front door. He came out on the front steps of the house, waving the gun; then he went back in. I kept turning my head back to watch him as my mother kept yanking my arm, telling me to run faster.

We went to a friend's house. For more than an hour, my mother was sobbing to this neighbor while the woman's husband was at our house trying to calm down my father. I kept straining to listen for any sounds of gunfire. The neighbor returned and said my father was better.

My feelings were very confused at this point. I began to think I hated my father for making my mother suffer. I had seen him violent and even wondered if he were crazy. My mother would say something was wrong with his brain from being hit too much as a boxer.

I was afraid to return home. Walking down the sidewalk, I looked from side to side at people peering out their windows. I felt embarrassed. At least the police hadn't been called!

From that day on, I never felt real security in my own home. I never had the courage to lift the top of the double sink, but I would often stare at it and wonder about the gun that lay beneath. Often my mother would tell me how my father almost beat a man to death on the street in Brooklyn, and I would wonder if he would kill somebody at work. Many times coming home from school, if I did not immediately see my mother, I wondered if she were lying dead in some room, having been shot by my father. I never shared these thoughts, but they were common.

I know all of this affected my picture of God at this age. While my mother kept talking of God's love, I had put together the name *God the Father* with my own father, so I struggled to believe God genuinely loved me and that that love wouldn't be mixed with hurt. Perhaps my mistrust of fathers, and the abounding religious superstition in my home, is why God had to pursue me in very private and personal ways. I suppose, as with every personal encounter with God, it doesn't matter if it makes sense to anyone but the person God is trying to communicate to.

In the summer of 1951, when I was six years old, I was sitting on the freshly seeded grass of our back yard one day, when I looked up and saw a wild rabbit sitting about twenty-five feet away. It hopped closer and then came within my reach. I remember looking around, appreciating the flowers, the warmth of the sun, and in particular the beauty of this little creature. Suddenly, I became aware that I too was a little creature that had a loving God who cared about me personally. He had created me and knew me. As a child, I shared this story with no one, yet I would think back on it often, assuring myself that if God cared for this rabbit, he cared about me too.

I suppose the way my mother overprotected me was a part of God's plan as well, instead of a great negative. Though her comments against my father clearly weren't good for my relationship with him, they showed me the ravages of gambling and as a result I was never once attracted to it.

Instead, I shared my mother's fantasy that someday my father would win so much money that he would stop gambling altogether. I can now see that his gambling was an illness and that he probably never would have stopped. Yet I lived in the hope that one day his luck would change . . . and that our one day a year together at the zoo would extend into many days together. I was too frightened by him and too fragile to be able to tell him any of this, and I don't know if it would have made a difference. All I could do was look forward to our priest's annual visit to our home. Perhaps his blessing would bring an end to the arguments and trouble.

Chapter 4

ADOLESCENCE

ONE DAY WHEN I WAS THIRTEEN, I STOOD BEHIND THE LARGE wooden bar in our home, mixing drinks for my relatives—my special chore for the last five years. It was a Saturday-evening party. As I was checking the bartender's guide for a drink unfamiliar to me, I heard the phone ring. A new priest from the local church was calling for an appointment to see our family.

It wasn't time for the yearly visit, and so the nature of the visit puzzled me. Several days later Father Valker arrived, not to bless us and exchange pleasantries but to focus on me. He questioned my parents as to why I, a thirteen-year-old, was not attending church, had not received catechism instruction, and had not received my first communion when most children received it at age seven.

My father was silent while my mother made excuses, but Father Valker was persistent. By the time the brief visit had ended, my parents had agreed that on Saturday mornings I would receive private catechism instruction from the priest.

And that was the beginning of the vast influence the church would have on me. How it would affect my choices and my views throughout young adulthood! Everything about the Catholic

Church was awe-inspiring and amazing to a gawky, insecure teen badly in need of guidance—any guidance. And did I ever take to what Catholicism offered me!

I arrived at the church early that first Saturday morning and found the whole experience intimidating. The first hurdle was simply getting through the front door. There was a two-way mirrored window and an intercom. When I pressed the doorbell, a woman's voice with a heavy German accent belted over the speaker, "Who is it? What do you want?"

"I am here to see Father Valker," I replied sheepishly.

She did not answer. I was startled by the sound of the loud, electronic buzz but did not know enough to reach to open the door at the sound. She buzzed it again and finally bellowed over the speaker, "Open the door!"

She had me sit in the reception area, flanked by photographs of Cardinal Stritch and Pope Pius XII. I stared forward at the stone staircase down which she said the priest would come. I heard the door close at the top of the stairs and soon saw Father Valker descending, wearing a long, black robe—a cassock—with a black sash around his waist.

In his bare office, he gave me a Baltimore Catechism, our study guide. Learning formal doctrine was a new experience for me. Questions familiar to Catholic and Protestant children alike (Who created man? Why did God create us? What is the chief purpose of man?) were totally foreign to me.

Father Valker was patient with my lack of knowledge. He seemed to have a parental concern for me. One Saturday he invited me to go with him and the altar boys to a baseball game. I appreciated the attention he gave me but felt inferior to the younger boys; they had so much more religious knowledge.

In order to receive communion, I first had to receive the sacrament of penance, known as confession. Before approaching the confessional on the scheduled day, I had written a long list of sins I had committed during my life. Sharing that list was not the thing that frightened me. I was far more afraid of the atmosphere surrounding the confessional, the anticipation of going into that small, dark, claustrophobic box. The red light indicated that someone else was in there; when it turned green, my heart rate increased. I entered the dark, hot box and knelt on the kneeling bench.

Although the sliding door was closed to the screen in front of me, I could clearly hear the confession of the person on the other side of the priest. I put my hands over my ears so I couldn't commit a new sin by listening to someone else's confession. When the wooden door slid open, I didn't hear it. I'm not sure how many times the priest spoke before I responded. I listed all my sins and listened to his reply. The penance he imposed was benevolent. This first visit to confession was the beginning of many visits. Throughout the years, I would grow in my desire to pay for my sins.

Now that I'd attended confession, I was ready for communion. I remembered stories of how important first communion was in Sicily and Little Italy. My first communion seemed equally important: It was the first time I could ever recall seeing both my parents in church at the same time.

The mass was still performed entirely in Latin in those days, so I followed the English translation in a missal. There was an air of mysticism as I watched the back of the priest, who performed an ancient rite with the elements of bread and wine. Coming from a family that taught me to appreciate the arts, especially music, and who had a flair for dramatics and custom, the mass strongly communicated to me the presence of a mysterious and powerful God.

From large stained-glass windows, sunlight was bathing the altar and the priest with colored light. On the marble steps in front of the priest, two altar boys were kneeling, one swinging a metal cylinder containing incense that sent clouds of smoke curling into the streams of the light. As the red, blue and orange smoke formed patterns, one alter boy would ring the Sanctus bells. The organ slowly crescendoed during the consecration, especially at the moment when the priest bent over the white hosts, saying in Latin, *"Hoc est enim Corpus meum."* Simultaneously, I read the translation: "This is my body." As he elevated the large host, a stream of golden light hit it.

By the mysterious and inexplicable powers of the priest, Jesus Christ was now truly present. I believed it, and I felt it. The priest said the words of an ancient rite over the cup of wine, which turned it into the blood of Christ. Only the priest would drink from the cup, but the sight of him gently lifting the bright golden chalice into the sunlight is one I treasured. I had a sense of God being mysterious and hidden but also personal as I received the communion wafer. Though I was caught up in the legalism of fasting and what to say in response to the priest, my overriding desire was to have an intimate union with God while the sacred host remained in my body.

And that dramatic experience was only the beginning of the church's effect on me during my teen years. Especially since high school was such a time of change in my life. Beginning high school, I was a tall, skinny boy with dark, curly hair. I had been part of a small, tight group of friends growing up. Mainly we played school and I was the teacher, or we had a local circus in which I played a magician. For many years, I never ventured off my block. I was never involved with the rougher group, the athletes, who were the mischief makers. As a result, I was a shy and easily intimidated young boy, the victim of every lunch-money hustler.

The first days in high school, I clutched my schedule, searching desperately for rooms. Every tough kid used the opportunity to send me in the wrong direction. On my way to the instrumental music department, I got sidetracked by a young prankster who sent me to the chlorine room of the swimming pool, where I intruded on a couple in the throes of romance. Having no sisters, this was the first girl I ever saw in her bra. Not wanting to seem like a voyeur, I held my class schedule in front of my eyes and asked the couple if they knew the way to the band room. The young man's response was not polite. When I did arrive at the music department, I was fifteen minutes late.

That's when I first saw him—Sig Swanson, the director of music. He was a man who would leave an indelible impression on me and literally change the course and direction of my life.

A tall, broad-shouldered Norwegian with wavy, blond hair, Sig Swanson was not only a gifted musician but also a teacher with genuine love for his students. He was very special to me, because for four years and some years after graduation he was a continual source of encouragement. He became my father figure when I desperately needed one. Looking back, I am sure he knew that something was wrong with my family, but he never mentioned it to me. With my commitment to keeping family secrets, this was probably the best course he could have taken.

To understand fully the impact Sig Swanson had on my life, it's necessary to understand the way other school officials viewed me. At best, I was an average student during my elementary years, usually struggling in the primary subjects. I didn't know anyone in my family who had ever gone to college, and no one had ever said I should break the trend. As the freshman counselor at East Leyden High School pored over my past grades, factoring in the prospects of this largely blue-collar community, he set me on a course of industrial arts even before I signed up for my first high-school class. Made up of metal shop, wood working, electrical wiring and leather making, the industrial-arts track sounded better than it was.

I wasn't eager to take college-bound courses, so the industrial arts looked fine to me. But I *did* want to take up a musical instrument. Although both my parents played musical instruments, and both of my older brothers had been given lessons when they were younger, I had no musical training during my elementary years and I missed it. But right before elementary-school graduation, I had heard the school band play the Percy Faith song, "A Theme from a Summer Place." To me, this seemed like the finest music I'd ever heard.

The band's rendition was probably filled with screeching woodwinds and an assortment of missed or wrong notes, but it motivated me to ask to take beginning band. How God used that simple choice! I remember the counselor doing everything he could to talk me out of it, but I see so clearly now how God was directing me toward band so that he could use the music teacher in my life.

It was soon obvious that I had no natural musical talent. If I wanted to play an instrument, I'd have to work! So I would arrive early in the morning and stay late after school practicing the cornet. I think that's what first caught Sig's attention—my determination to put so much energy into a task. Perhaps I was also looking for his attention, and if he understood that, he responded. He began by giving me duties, first as the music librarian, then as the uniform custodian. Always, my main motivation was to please him.

Soon I began a pattern of waiting on the steps of the music department before school opened. From those outside steps I could see his home and watch as he walked toward school. He always had a cheerful hello for me in the morning. For someone as starved for affection as I was, especially from a male figure, it wasn't surprising how much effect little things could have. Periodically, he would invite me to his home for lunch. His wife treated me like a stepson. I began to feel worthy of attention.

No matter what I did in high school, he praised me—even if the project wasn't related to the music department. My junior year I worked on the soundtrack for a slide show on gangs. He said it was great! In between numbers, he would tell the whole band how impressed he was by the audio-visual.

Each year he and his assistant, Dick Jacoby, would go to the Sherman House in downtown Chicago for an annual music conference. One year they took me along. Together we rode the elevated train, went through the exhibit area and sat in on the day's clinics. I was overwhelmed by their attention.

In some ways, my growth during those four years of high school was like that of a flower trying to push through barren and dry soil. What I became after four years bore little resemblance to what I was when I began school.

But through all the changes, I continued with all my religious devotions, including spraying holy water on the bed each night and wearing holy medals. These were things I kept largely to myself.

My increase in religious practices probably had a direct relationship with my family dynamics. Things were changing, and not for the better. My father and I had no relationship during my high-school years. He worked for a shoe company in downtown Chicago, and by the time he came home from work and ate alone (we rarely ate together as a family), he would fall asleep in front of the television set. He spent all day on Saturday and some evenings at the racetrack.

The distance between us was not all his fault. I never asked him about his work. I had outgrown trips to the zoo and had no desire to go to the racetrack with him. At this age, I was still angry with him for what I believe he had inflicted on my mother and for blacklisting relatives I cared about.

The little family stability that was there was also eroding. My brother Anthony was nineteen, still living at home and working at a local factory. One day he announced that he was an atheist. At this point, I had formulated such a clear picture of who would go to heaven and who would go to hell that I feared for the loss of his eternal life. I would argue with him from the catechism, and he would respond with Aristotle and Socrates. His loss of faith was an event that really floored me. I loved him and couldn't contemplate his not going to heaven. My mother cried, my brother and I argued, and my father remained silent.

I was so concerned that I went to see Father Valker and discussed it with him. He told me not to be alarmed, that he had dealt with such matters before. He gave me a special, blessed scapular and told me to conceal it under my brother's mattress. It was supposed to help bring my brother back to the faith. However, the years went on, and I saw no change in Anthony's attitude.

Also during my high-school years my brother Joe returned from the Navy, announcing that he would soon marry a woman he'd met in a San Diego bar. Her brother was a Carmelite priest. I was excited about the possibility of having a relative that was a priest, but the marriage only lasted a few months.

Joe and Mary had lots of arguments. Eventually Mary spent more and more time in a local bar while Joe was working. One day she went back to California. My brother couldn't get an annulment from the church until many years later, so he married again outside of the church.

The following year, my brother Anthony married too. His future mother-in-law wanted the wedding in a Lutheran church and the couple agreed. I had never stepped inside a Protestant church in my life, and I didn't know if I could. I went to Father Valker, who simply related the teaching at the time: never enter a Protestant church.

My mother and brothers insisted that no harm would come to me if I would sit in the church during the ceremony, yet the priest's instructions had been clear. This perhaps was one of the first actions I took that went against family tradition. Rather than disobey the Catholic Church, I remained on the front steps of the church throughout the wedding. My brothers were angry and my mother kept insisting that I come in, but I held my ground and would occasionally peek through the crack in the church door into the dimly lit sanctuary. Those were the first times I can remember my brothers calling me stupid or telling me my actions were ridiculous. I hadn't learned that church was to be flexible for family. Instead, I had become scrupulously religious.

Indeed, I was developing a secret religious life. Every day after school I would practice late in the music department and then walk home, because the bus left right after school. I'd arrive home after six o'clock every night. My mother assumed I'd been at school all that time, but I wasn't.

Until only a few years ago, I never told anyone where I'd spent the unaccounted-for hours. Most afternoons during high school, I would sit alone and unnoticed in a dark corner of the balcony of St. Gertrude's Church.

Sometimes I would kneel, sometimes I would sit, but mostly I would gaze at the large cross with the body of the crucified Christ on it that hung over the altar. I spent many days trying to figure out why Jesus died. No one had ever told me why. As I huddled in the darkness, I would pray, asking God to stop my father's gambling habit and to stop the quarreling at home. There in the silence I started to develop what I would only have a name for many years later, a desire to serve God.

From my balcony view I would watch people come and go, but they would never see me, and I wanted it that way. I liked it best when the church grew dark. Then the intensity of the flickering candles became almost mesmerizing. When I was sure that no one was around, I would make my way down from the balcony to the sanctuary floor. There I would kneel in front of the saints and light candles. It was a good, warm feeling. In the next half hour walking home, I would remember a specific candle I had lit and think that in some mysterious way it was continuing the prayer I had prayed before it.

There is something about that church balcony I will never forget. Though my theology was very misguided, God was inviting me on a journey. But my theology wouldn't let me just accept the invitation. In my heart, I knew I was not worthy to go to heaven. I believed in purgatory and knew I would have to be punished for a time in order to purify myself if I were ever to see God. My response was like that of most Catholics I knew, I would say that I would hope I would be with God someday or hope I would be in heaven, but I had no assurance of salvation.

That lack of certainty drove me to perform more and more works. To gain God's approval, I would purposely stay on my knees until they ached. I would say prayers and make the stations of the cross, especially if they included an indulgence, which basically would take time off my stay in purgatory. If I could get to heaven only by working off my sins, it meant I would have to work very hard indeed.

God certainly used Sig Swanson as an anchor during those years. Amid the family instability and my search for spiritual definition, Sig helped me develop positive self-esteem and healthy relationships. By the time I was a senior, I actually felt good about myself. That will sound like a strange thing to many, but as a shy and intimidated young man without a father giving me encouragement or a blessing, I didn't know if there was anything really good about me. It was almost miraculous that in my senior year I was voted the best male speaker in the school, when I had come in as a shy freshman.

By my senior year, I was taking care of project after project for the music department. Before a major concert, I would set the stage and for weeks before go door to door selling tickets. One day before a major concert my senior year, I was rehearsing with the band. An unexpected announcement came over the speaker telling us of President Kennedy's assassination. He was a president I greatly admired, probably the first president to have a real impact on me, and I was stunned. Sig looked out the window for the longest time, occasionally glancing back at the now-mute speaker. Then he raised his baton and asked us to start at letter G. I remember thinking that surely we couldn't go on with business as usual, that everything should come to a grinding halt. He said something that because of the moment has remained with me. "No matter how great, everyone can be replaced."

He went ahead with the concert and included some extra numbers as a memorial to the president. I hadn't thought much about dying before that moment, but as an adult I have surely come to understand the impact of Sig's words.

Sig did something the day after the concert that had a great effect on me. He had the cash receipts from the concert, over $2,000, in a canvas bank bag. He handed it to me and asked me to bring it to the bank. I must have looked paralyzed, because he repeated the instructions again and told me the deposit slip was enclosed with the money. I walked the five blocks to the bank, clutching the canvas bag tightly. What was going through my mind was not the fear of robbers, but one question: *Why does he trust me?* By the time I got back to school, it had translated into the thought, *I must be trustworthy, because he trusts me.* I don't know how deeply he thought about his actions, but it was one of those moments in which he showed me something in myself that I could not see without his help.

There is no question whatsoever in my mind that I went to college because of Sig Swanson. Although the high-school counselors didn't mean it, their message was, "You're not good enough." They tried their best to encourage me to get a high-paying factory job. Sig asked me quite simply one day what college I wanted to go to. When I told him I wasn't going to college, he balked, "What do you mean, you're not going to college? Of course, you are! You can do it."

These were the kind of statements that were a blessing to me. I was a trumpet and cello player working hard to keep up with peers that had real talent. I also worked hard in the last two years of high school to prepare for college. I was accepted at every college I applied to, and chose Elmhurst College, where I would be a music major. It was very painful to leave the nurturing, mentor relationship I had with Sig. I missed him as if he were my father.

And soon I found out in an agonizing way how much I needed a father. That summer between high school and college, I developed a painful, psychosomatic ulcer that eventually hospitalized me. The hospitalization set the stage for a most dramatic family event. Our family physician was an aging Italian woman named Marie LaGoble. We had a family conference to discuss my medical condition. My mother insisted that I was merely eating the wrong foods, but the doctor knew it was more than that. In the process of trying to explain what a psychosomatic illness was, Dr. LaGoble turned to my father and said, "When are you going to be a father to this boy?"

I felt the blood drain out of my head. My father was not used to being questioned directly by anyone, no less a woman.

"I don't know what you mean," he retorted.

My mother's eyes never left the floor. Apparently, she had talked to the doctor in private, and although a general practitioner, Dr. LaGoble had formed a clear picture of our home life. She kept pushing my father, "When was the last time you had a conversation with your son? What do you know of his interests and activities?"

He shifted nervously in his seat. Then she brought up the family secret, the thing that could not be talked about outside of the home. She talked about my father's gambling.

He cut her off in mid-sentence: "That's none of your business!"

But she did not back down. Finally, capturing my father's attention, she said, "I want to ask you this one important question. Which is more important to you: your son or the horses?"

My father did not take any time to think, but replied forcefully, "Horses!"

I look back with praise to God for how he balanced two opposing forces at that point in my life: my father's rejection and Sig Swanson's love. The doctor suggested that it might have been better for me to be removed from my home when I was younger. The effect of my father's rejection statement could have been a deadly blow—especially for the fearful, frail, intimidated, quiet boy I had been before Sig Swanson had given me self-respect, the courage to pursue goals and the belief that I was important, at least to him.

My private church time had prepared me too. Although I had become very legalistic and ritualistic in my religious practices, I think God's Spirit was inviting me to know him. I can't say that at the time I had a personal relationship with God, for he still seemed distant and capricious to me, but I believe he was setting the stage for a relationship to come. A relationship that would bring the healing I needed.

Chapter 5

COLLEGE

I WAS FULL OF EXCITEMENT AS I CARRIED LUGGAGE INTO NIEBUHR Hall at Elmhurst College, in a Chicago suburb. Only in the last two years had Sig convinced me that I could even *go* to college. I knew this first year would be a struggle academically, because I hadn't taken the college prep classes other students had. But I wouldn't mind the work. It felt wonderful knowing that I didn't have to make do with being a factory worker all my life; maybe God had bigger plans for me.

I soon realized that I'd have to adjust to school life on many levels—not just academics. Though there were no bullies to contend with here, as there were in those first days of high school, there was a strong Protestant undercurrent that I hadn't anticipated.

When I chose to go to Elmhurst, it was because of its strong music program. I hadn't even noticed that the college was tied to a religious denomination. It turned out that Elmhurst College had been a proseminary in its origin and was still related to the United Church of Christ. Many of my classmates were Bible majors who would be going on to Protestant seminaries. Some had fathers who were pastors or parents who were missionaries. I couldn't relate to any of it.

I was one of the few Roman Catholic students on campus and the only one singing in the choir, a requirement for music majors. I loved the choir but dreaded the times we sang in Protestant churches. I felt that I was obligated to go, but it was just so foreign to me. In fact, the college chapel was the first Protestant church I ever stepped into. The first time that everyone abruptly turned toward the altar and began singing the doxology, I wondered what was going on. That wasn't something we'd gone over in choir practice. Uneasy that I was betraying the one true faith, I kept a rosary in my pocket and would often say my own prayers during the service.

Of course, it didn't take me long to find a place where I could meet with God. A path from my dorm through Wilder Park led to a Catholic church that became the substitute for my home-church balcony. Almost every evening I was able to find a time to sit there and pray when the church was quiet and vacant. I felt a lot of uncertainty and confusion about where I was really going in life and so would often ask for God to send me a sign.

Almost from the start of college, I began to question whether music was the right career for me. I enjoyed it but knew I probably was a music major more out of admiration for Sig than for any other reason. I knew God would have plans for my future, so I hoped he would speak to me, perhaps by making the tabernacle light get just a shade brighter or by shaking the tabernacle veil. I had read so much about saints receiving signs. All I asked for was a tiny one, but nothing ever happened.

In spring, I had to have even more contact with Protestant ways. The choir went on tour to the East Coast by way of Canada, through New England, then New York, Pennsylvania and Ohio. We were only gone for the week of spring break, but leaving the sanctuary and security of the church across the park made me nervous.

So did the concerts held in Protestant churches. One time I was putting on my choir robe in a Michigan church when I noticed two ceramic wall plaques of Martin Luther and John Calvin. Immediately I looked away. I knew very little about the Reformation, but I did know it was wrong. According to my theology, these two men were heretics paying for their sins in hell. What was I doing in a place that honored them? When the pastor joined us, I blocked out the words of his prayer, worried that it might be wrong to listen.

I studied each Protestant church we sang in. None of them had a red tabernacle light; that told me the presence of God was absent. The plain cross—without the body of the crucified Christ—seemed empty and barren. From what I could see, the Protestant faith seemed too easy. It lacked discipline—no penance, no kneeling for hours, especially no sense of urgency to do the things that would get one to heaven. My classmates were just good people on the wrong road.

I knew heaven was something that you had to work for. I sensed that there was something about me that was good enough if I worked at it, and it would enable me to go to heaven. I had yet to confront the God that the apostle Paul spoke of in Romans.

I suppose I appeared strange to my peers on the choir tour. I did things that wouldn't have made sense to them. Normally, we slept in the homes of church families. One evening I opted to sleep on the wooden pew in the balcony of a church. In doing so, I missed both dinner and breakfast. Not surprisingly, the church was very cold at night and the wooden pew uncomfortable. It seemed a necessary self-imposed penance.

Another time, in Detroit, I saw a Catholic church several blocks from the church we were to sing in. I felt the urge to go to confession. With my choir robe still on, I went several blocks to the church and waited in line at the confessional door. The priest gave me a particularly long penance of prayers. As I said the prayers, the time of the concert drew nearer and nearer. I would be missed if I didn't make the concert because I played both the trumpet and English hand bells, as well as sang with the larger group. Worried that I would be late, I ran the blocks back to the church, my blue choir robe billowing in the wind. I ran up a back flight of stairs and joined the choir just as they entered the risers. Though I was panting, I felt better, knowing I'd needed the purification which came from the priest's absolution.

The Catholic/Protestant issue wasn't the only one that captured my concern. Back on campus, I was elected to the student government, and I listened intently to my classmates talking about the need for social change. Since President Kennedy's assassination, these were, of course, times of particular social upheaval. Cities were literally burning. Martin Luther King, Jr., was working for civil rights for blacks in Chicago. (My father thought that he was largely a troublemaker.)

Not knowing God's Word, I didn't understand God's thirst for social justice. But I had an inward sense of what was right, and especially what was wrong. News coverage of blacks being hit with fire hoses and bitten by police dogs, churches being bombed—such sights shook me from apathy.

While a delegation from our school went to Selma, Alabama, I marched with a group of students through our college town. It was a cold and windy day as we reached the steps of the city hall. My English professor, Dr. Couchman, gave an eloquent speech about justice and equality. By the end of his speech, his red hair was covered with white snow. One could see his every breath as he spoke into the megaphone. His leadership intrigued me. From our times together in class, I hadn't known he was a Christian, but when the time came, he spoke boldly and courageously.

I hadn't wanted to risk marching in Selma, but when the college president asked me to represent Elmhurst College to an all-black college in Austin, Texas, I said yes. I was going as a student-government leader, and it was basically a public-relations trip where I would speak to their student government and in a school assembly. I was able to hitch a ride with two students who were Texas natives.

This trip would be another turning point in my life. Up until then, I was so busy telling God who he should be in my life, that God didn't have the chance to tell me who *he* wanted to be. What began as a very simple trip would be used by God to gain my attention in a powerful way.

After a rather long drive from Elmhurst, Illinois, snaking

through the Ozark Mountains, we pulled into an Arkansas gas station about midnight. A young man in coveralls leaned back in a chair against the wooden frame of the building. He didn't move. He just looked at us. I got out of the back seat to stretch and put money in a pop machine for a Coke. Moving in what seemed like slow motion, he eventually started pumping gas and said to me, "Where y'all from?"

"Chicago," I responded quickly.

"What brings y'all down here?" he continued.

Rather than speaking for my companions who were going home, I just spoke for myself. I was proud of this official mission and informed him how I was representing my Northern college to an all-black college in Austin, Texas. He made no verbal response—just bit his lower lip and brushed his unshaven cheek with the back of his hand.

When we pulled away from the station, I was in the front passenger seat, given the duty of keeping the driver awake. We were in Texarkana, Arkansas, winding through a dark forest. The only light came from our auto. I was just falling asleep when we rounded a curve, and I caught a glimpse of an auto on the shoulder of the road. I looked in the side mirror and noticed that the headlights came on as soon as we passed. The car then pulled onto the road abruptly. Its brights were on, and it was gaining speed on us. Suddenly we noticed a car coming toward us with its brights on too.

Our driver alternated his lights, but the other auto didn't respond. Then with a gasp of profanity, the driver said, "My God, we're going to have a head on! He's in our lane!" The student in back bolted from his sleep. I braced my knees against the glove compartment. Our driver hit his brakes, swerving to the right to avoid the oncoming auto. We plunged off the road a few feet, barely missing several trees. My fright increased. The car that had been following us, followed us off the road and hit our back bumper intentionally. Every time our driver started to brake, the car behind would hit our back bumper and force us deeper into the forest.

We stopped a good distance from the highway, the bright lights of both autos on us. I thought we were going to be robbed and wanted to put my wallet under the floor mat, but there wasn't any time. I saw the large figure of a man come up to my window. He tapped something metal on the glass. *Oh, my God,* I thought to myself when I looked at the large barrel of a silver revolver.

There were other men, four in all, cursing at us to get out of the car. My seat belt jammed. The more I struggled to get it off, the more edgy this armed man became. Finally, it unclasped, and he pulled me by the collar and threw me against the hood of the car. I began to ask for an explanation. He just said, "Shut up!"

The next time I tried to talk, he hit me with his metal flashlight. My traveling companions were also straddled against the front hood of the car opposite me. In a sense, each of us would have a unique and individual experience, depending on which man was handling us.

A guy with a large pot belly, chewing tobacco, stood his distance. He was the one the others looked to for direction. They were all wearing the same clothes, khaki brown shirts and pants, and large black boots. There was no reference to why they were treating us this way. For nearly an hour they joked about what they should do with us.

Then we were ordered to take off our shoes. The man who held me captive tore out the liners. I was then ordered to take off my pants and hand them to this gruff guy. He turned the pockets inside out, throwing loose change, bills and my rosary on the hood. The strip search was in no way gentle. The metal of the automobile felt very cold against my body, although the air was warm and humid. Before the man who held me had completed his body search, he touched me in a place I didn't want to be touched, which made me lose my breath. I felt weak inside, and humiliated.

We were allowed to put our clothes back on, but no sooner had we done this than one of the students was brought into the forest, out of our sight. A minute later he let out a scream. My body instantly tensed. For a moment, I felt myself losing control of my bladder. I thought my friend had been stabbed, but I later learned that he had been kicked in the groin and had doubled over onto the ground.

Then the big man standing at a distance began asking each of us what we had done with the wedding ring we had found in the washroom of the gas station. Of course, we didn't know what he was talking about. Two of the guys went in the car and began stripping our upholstery. The inside of the car was a mess. He then opened the trunk and pulled clothes out of suitcases, throwing them on the ground. He looked in the engine too but didn't probe.

Then I realized I had said too much back at the gas station because the next question was, "Which one of you Northern boys is coming down here to help the niggers?"

None of us said anything. We got a lecture on Southerners not needing any help from Northerners in controlling the "Negro population." I started thinking about the three young civil rights activists who had been killed recently. Would that be our fate? These men were all much larger than we were. I knew it was complete folly to think of running away or overpowering them. It was now three o'clock in the morning in the pitch-black forest. No one would be able to see or hear us from the highway.

I knew that we were going to be killed.

We would be killed and perhaps never found. I felt completely helpless—that was the most frightening feeling of all.

Knowing we'd be murdered soon, I began some hard thinking, but I didn't think about my family or my school. I thought about God and in one sense really felt his presence.

At times the men would harass us, and at other times they would go off and speak quietly among themselves. During one of those pauses, I made an Act of Contrition, the prayer a Catholic says after confession or in the face of imminent death. My body ached from the rough treatment. I was nineteen, and it seemed to me too young to die.

While the leader regrouped his men, who all followed his lead by putting their thumbs in their belts, chewing tobacco and spitting on the ground, I was motivated by desperation to say something to God that was totally sincere: "If there is any way you can get me out of this, I will go where you want me to go and do what you want me to do for the rest of my life."

Suddenly and abruptly, as daybreak came, the leader told us to get on our way and never come through Texarkana again. We were stunned but got in the car and skidded onto the highway. We'd been in that forest almost seven hours.

The two automobiles followed us down the winding road, and we were all still nervous. Then about a half an hour later we quickly pulled into the gravel parking lot of a restaurant. The two other cars continued up the road. I'll never forget those two white autos each with a brown star and the word *Marshall* on the door. We'd been held captive by the local police!

None of us ate. I tried to sip coffee with shaking hands.

When I arrived at Huston-Tillotson College, I went immediately to President Seabrook's office and told him what had happened. He showed obvious concern but looked at me soberly and replied, "You were lucky. Sometimes guests coming to see us end up in a lockup for more than a week, and we have to get the FBI to find them."

What had happened was a nice job of harassment in a charged racial atmosphere.

I had been the victim of a crime during those hours when I was held against my will, struck and intimidated with a gun. I had been given cause to fear for my life. Yet it was a kind of coming of age for me, of seeing evil in the world in its raw form. And God was not going to let me forget what I had said to him. From that time on, my promise would come to my mind every time I had an important choice to make in my life.

Up until this point, religion had been a safe and secure place for me. But now, even without knowing the Bible, I was realizing the cost of following God. Because the world seemed an ever more frightening place, this would have an impact on decisions I would make in the next few years.

My week at the all-black college was eye opening. I will never

forget the evening some of us went to eat at a local restaurant.
No one would serve us. When I demanded attention, the waitress
threw the utensils on our table. The black students were eager
to leave; I just wasn't getting the hang of how the system worked.

Returning to my own campus, I got more involved in politics
and became interested in Lyndon Johnson's war on poverty. What
kept haunting me was my suburban upbringing and my igno-
rance of the poverty and the conditions of the inner city of Chicago. I can't even explain today the forces that drove me to
witness poverty firsthand.

A part-time maintenance job during the school year and a government loan were putting me through school, so I felt I could
afford to devote my summer to experiencing the hardships of the
inner city. While I told my mother I was working at the college
that summer, I spent almost every day somewhere in Chicago. I
would take the elevated train to a neighborhood that looked bad
and then get off the train. I realize now how dangerous this was.
I was in a different gang's territory almost every week, gangs like
the Vice Lords and the Egyptian Cobras. I spent hours with alco-
holics on what was then called skid row. All I'd do was listen.
Then I would sit on the front step of a black tenement, listening
to an old black man or a young Hispanic.

It wasn't research the way a sociologist would do it. I simply
wanted to learn more about this world. A college friend of mine,
Bernie, knew what I was doing and asked to come down to the
city one day. We went together, and that evening a dozen gang
members surrounded us, pushing and shoving. The leader
slapped me across the face and told us to start running. After we
did, they threw rocks which hit us in the back.

Out on the street, people I talked to often got abusive. They
were always unpredictable. One evening, while crossing a bridge
overpass, a derelict pulled out a straight razor and put it to my
neck. He eventually put it away and said he'd only been kidding,
but those were terrifying moments.

Yet, I kept going back. Sometimes I would sleep at the Union
train station. A cop would inevitably hit me on the feet with a billy

club and tell me to get out. I would go without eating for up to three days, which I could hardly take. My head would be pounding. This is the way some people lived every day of their lives.

As the summer went on, I developed better strategies. I would wear old clothes, not shave, even smudge my face with burnt cork. During the last month, I would hide my father's 8mm camera under my coat and film a lot of what I saw.

I don't think I was trying to impress others because hardly anyone knew I was doing it. It was just something I thought I had to do—regardless of who understood. When school started again, I shared the film and my experiences in a college-newspaper article. A few appreciated my perspective, some said nothing, a lot thought I was stupid.

In many ways, I was pulling into myself, becoming more introspective. I would only date girls if they'd want to talk about poverty or world suffering, and that rather limited my social life. I spent a lot of time pacing in a cemetery near the college chapel. At the same time, I was increasing my private spiritual ritual. In that Catholic church across the park I would sometimes stay on my knees for two or three hours, even walk on my knees in the sanctuary. As I look back, I was simply trying to get a clear sign from God as to what I should do with my life.

No one was ever in the church to witness me, or so I thought. One evening, a nun came up to me and told me that she had been watching me many evenings. "Your piety is rare for someone your age," she said.

The next day she invited me to her convent, which was adjacent to the church. While I sat in the parlor, she brought me a small monstrance which contained a fragment of a bone from St. Agatha, the saint this order of nuns followed. I didn't realize it at the time, but in showing me and allowing me to kiss the relic, she was giving me a privilege rarely given to outsiders.

Eventually, I came to know these nuns very well. I would sit in the sewing room while the older nuns were repairing habits and talk about religious things. One day one of the older nuns said, "Truly, God has a special purpose for you."

It felt good to hear that, but I couldn't imagine what that purpose might be.

The following week, the Mother Superior said, "Many of the sisters believe you are called of God."

She told me to meet Father Heining at the rectory. I scheduled a meeting and without much conversation he said, "God may be calling you to be a priest."

That was something that had never entered my mind.

He said, "You must go to the seminary. If it is not God's will, he will let you know."

At the seminary I was interviewed by the rector, Father Roger Kaffer, a short, balding, pear-shaped priest with sparkling eyes and an infectious smile. He accepted me as a candidate for the Roman Catholic priesthood at St. Charles Borromeo Seminary.

I would, of course, continue college in the seminary, but I didn't know if leaving Elmhurst was the right thing. I finally made the decision one day while pacing in the small cemetery on the college property.

My mother was excited by the news. My father remained silent. But my brothers were more outspoken. One said, "What's wrong with you? Don't you like girls?"

The summer before entering seminary, I went to New York with my parents. That would prove to be the last time we would all be together.

Though for me Brooklyn was only a nice place to visit, it meant very different things to each of my family members. For my mother, these returns were always painful as they were a reminder of her quasi-captivity in New York. My brothers, Joe and Tony, remembered the scenes of their early childhoods. The large brownstones hadn't really changed much since my father was a boy there either. I wonder what those visits were like for him.

I enjoyed walking through the Brooklyn neighborhoods my father had been raised in. But I saw grim reflections of the old days. One day we were in the second-floor apartment of my father's sister, my aunt Tessie. There was a phone call. She shrieked, called my father to the phone, and we all soon discovered that Uncle Lou, my father's brother, was going to shoot his wife.

My father rushed out the door while Tessie half cried and exchanged gossip. I slowly realized that these calls were a weekly affair. My father's younger brother Lou had my father's temper. By day he worked as a mechanic. In the evening, he and his wife went ballroom dancing. But occasionally they would have fights so fierce that they could be heard down the block. Oddly enough, though Lou threatened his wife with bodily harm, he never touched her. He probably had learned the same code of conduct that my father had: Never hit a woman. I learned years later that Uncle Lou was really a gentle man.

I see now that among my motives for wanting to become a priest was a hope that as a priest I would bring some sense of peace and harmony to the family. I could see myself coming to weddings and parties and somehow representing God. Not that it was a very realistic idea. My family needed far more help than my occasional visits would give them.

Helping my family was only one of my motives, of course. Only years later did I realize that there was a lot of escapism mixed in with the decision. The world, with its social upheaval and the experience in the Arkansas forest, was a frightening place. My home life too was unsettling, and while I didn't really feel a call to celibacy, it was hard for me to picture myself in a good marriage when I'd never seen one lived out. By now I was married to religiosity and ritual; that seemed more comfortable to me than investing in risky relationships.

Everybody in New York and then Chicago bade me good-by the way they had Joe when he went into the Navy. Only this wasn't for several years; this was for life.

Chapter 6

SEMINARY

MY FIRST VISIT TO THE ROMAN CATHOLIC SEMINARY WAS NEARLY a disaster. I had received an engraved invitation to a formal dinner which was the installation of the new bishop. Apart from seeing Cardinal Stritch as a child, I had never met a bishop. Before the dinner there would be the elaborate installation ceremony in the large cathedral. Knowing it was a formal occasion, I decided to rent a tuxedo. Making a good impression would be vital. I wanted to start my seminary career off right.

When I arrived at the cathedral, another man dressed in a tuxedo told me to stand at a curb and open the door of each limousine that arrived. I was greatly honored although unsure why I'd been singled out. Apparently, the local Knights of Columbus also were wearing tuxedos, and I had been mistaken for a knight.

Suddenly, a large, black limousine pulled up. I immediately opened the back door and found Cardinal Cody of Chicago, the highest ranking bishop, referred to as the metropolitan for the diocese. As he stepped out, he held his hand inches from my face. Thinking he was showing me his large, emerald ring, I commented, "It's very nice."

The man next to me poked me in the ribs and whispered loudly, "Kiss it." He then knelt, pulling me down to kneel also.

The Cardinal didn't seem to notice my errors.

After my initial faux pax, I sat in the balcony and watched a most impressive ceremony. The choir sang beautifully as the magnificently dressed concelebrants and abbots processed down the wide main aisle. Finally came the bishops, with their tall, pointed hats.

The ceremony had some of the wonder of my first communion. To this day, I believe that one of the most meaningful liturgies in Christendom is the placing of a large, open Bible on the back of the kneeling bishop, signifying the weight and authority of God's Word.

After the ceremony was over, the church bells rang as the new bishop stepped out of the front doors of the cathedral, holding his shining gold staff.

When I arrived at the dining hall of the new seminary, I went from table to table looking for a place card with my name on it. The rector came over to me and told me I would be working in the kitchen. Apparently, I had misunderstood. I was not a guest but a server!

I quickly removed my tuxedo jacket, rolled up my sleeves and began scooping food onto plates in the hot, steamy kitchen. Sometime later, I was washing my hands in the restroom when a fellow who would be in seminary with me, Mike Coleman, introduced himself. He looked at my pleated shirt and the satin stripe on my black pants and did everything to hold back laughter.

With an infectious smile, he said, "Did you *really* think you were going to eat with *them?*"

I nodded, and we both laughed. I had not come up through the ranks as an altar boy or as a minor seminarian, and it certainly showed. Every other seminarian knew the formal invitation had been a courtesy gesture of the rector's and reported directly to the kitchen!

As I left, I almost bumped into a priest who was visibly inebriated. He put his arm on my shoulder and said in slurred words, "Always be obedient, young man. Never, never question Holy Mother Church."

That priest was one of the few I ever met with a drinking problem, though I would meet more priests who gave obedience to a seemingly monolithic institution—Holy Mother Church. But most of the priests I would meet would be very stable, intelligent people, many with an undeniably strong personal relationship with Jesus.

I would have to choose as well what kind of priest I would be. And since the night of my promise to God in that dark Arkansas forest, I was committed to going wherever God wanted me to go. To me this was the essence of obedience.

* * *

My father asked me to take a ride with him the day before I entered the seminary. I could tell he wanted an opportunity to talk. As he looked straight forward, seeming to concentrate fully on his driving, he said, "Are you sure you know what you're doing?" It wasn't accusatory. He simply added, "You know priests are men just like anyone else. There's politics in the church too."

I thought he was wrong there. Even after meeting the intoxicated priest, I still believed that all priests were special, almost perfect.

The next day I entered St. Charles Borromeo Seminary, in Lockport, Illinois. That first day of my new vocation, I knelt in the chapel, looking at the stained-glass windows depicting the seven steps to the priesthood. It would be at least three years before I would be ordained a cleric during a tonsure ceremony. It seemed so far away.

But there were many new aspects to seminary life that I felt I was making progress toward the priesthood. Most of my priestly images had come from movie characters, such as Gregory Peck in *Keys of the Kingdom* and Bing Crosby in *Going My Way*. Since I had never been an altar boy, I had never worn clerical garments before. Once I was in the seminary, I was given a cassock to wear. It was a long, black garment with many buttons, a Roman collar and a sash with a tassel on the side. Wearing the cassock helped me feel religious. Although I didn't have to wear religious garments all the time, I enjoyed wearing the cassock as much as I could. I abandoned most of the clothes I wore in college in place of a black clergy shirt and black pants.

The seminary was a highly disciplined environment. We got up early, usually at six-thirty, for morning prayers and then attended classes in Latin and church history and philosophy. Seminarians took turns serving at the daily mass. I enjoyed it and would volunteer as often as possible.

The evening meal was always formal. We stood at attention as the rector and his faculty marched into the dining hall and sat at the head table. After the blessing, we ate without loud conversation. Sometimes a priest would gesture to one of us, inviting that person to sit at the head table after dinner. I appreciated being chosen. Often there were birthday celebrations. On certain days, priests would read one of the accounts from the lives of the saints.

At night there was a period called the grand silence. From nine o'clock until the next morning, only essential conversation was permitted. As an Italian, I found that difficult. Another thing that seemed to go contrary to my Italian upbringing was speaking without using many hand gestures—which was considered too emotional. One day the rector came up to me from behind and grabbed my arms, saying, "Now talk!"

The seminarians, coming from all over the country, were a mixed breed. To me, most fit into two categories. To put it in my own vernacular, some were okay and some weren't. The ones that weren't okay were scrupulous, bookish, introverted, unconcerned with social issues and even effeminate. The ones that were okay were manly, concerned about social issues and able to see the humor in things.

I'll never forget one example of the contrast between the not okays and okays. At one dinner, a priest announced that Martin Luther King, Jr., had been assassinated. Spontaneously, one table of Southerners rose to their feet, cheering and applauding. The rector was upset and so was I.

Yet I was glad that everyone wasn't completely alike. The exposure to different professors and priests was good. There were the Christian brothers from both the Irish Christian and the French De La Salle groups. Few were ordained priests; most just belonged to the religious order. And then there were the Oblates of Mary Immaculate, who each wore a large, black crucifix, called a pectoral, tucked into the side of his sash. I was most intrigued by the Jesuits. They were considered the intelligentsia of the church, not being ordained until they were thirty-three years old. Jesuit Father Andrew Greeley, one of my teachers, was a prominent sociologist who went on to be an author well known in religious and nonreligious circles.

Another priest I respected was Father Kaffer. He had a good sense of humor. At times his body seemed to shake with laughter. He was the most dramatic priest as a celebrant. A devout and sincere man, he eventually became a bishop of the diocese. I liked him, although I wasn't sure if he ever really liked me. I never fit his image of a good seminarian. He had once called me a "kook" in a reference letter; he didn't intend for me to know this, but his secretary inadvertently put the letter in an envelope addressed to me.

In order to give seminarians close role models and to have specific persons guide our steps, we each were assigned a spiritual director. It was a good idea. My first mentor was Father Brown. Most of his religious advice centered on being more devoted to the Virgin Mary—a priority of his religious order, the Oblates of Mary Immaculate.

I liked Father Brown, though in some ways I found him humorous. I am sure he meant well the day I knocked on his partially opened door and before he responded he raced to a kneeler, wove his hands together, looked up at a crucifix on his wall and said, "Come in." Father Brown had come out of a school that believed in the importance of appearances.

One priest, Father Paul, was the seminary dean. He called me into his office one day and asked why he hadn't seen me in chapel more often, as he was in the habit of taking attendance. Since high-school days, I had developed a habit of praying in quiet and solitude, so I often entered the chapel at night and sat in a dark corner. I took offense with his need to know about my private devotion to God (especially since I was probably in the chapel more than most of my fellow seminarians), but I didn't let him know it. I conformed to his wishes and began going into the chapel at times when I would be seen. I was beginning to understand the importance of appearances to these priests.

As I look back, I realize I can only judge Father Brown, Father Paul and the rest of my teachers in light of the times in which they were trained. During my seminary years, I was on the edge of a new era in the church. The results of the Second Vatican Council were only beginning to show changes. The priests who were my teachers predominantly studied theology in the 1940s and 1950s. The ideas which I came to chafe at were strongly ingrained into them during their own religious upbringing.

But I didn't want to *pretend* to be religious. I wanted to live out my faith. I had higher standards for myself than anyone else did and was always looking for more devotion and penance to impose on myself. I would sign up for several tours of duty during any forty-hour devotion, although I never enjoyed kneeling on the hard marble floor. I would often fast through dinner in order to make the stations of the cross.

At this point in my life, I took everything seriously—my studies, my religious rituals and myself. Naturally, I judged any seminarians who didn't act like the mini-priest I was.

Oddly enough, my best friend was an improbable choice. He was Mike Coleman, the student who had laughed with me about the tuxedo. At first glance, Mike and I would not seem a good partnership; he wasn't into the "form" of religious life the way I was. But I was fascinated with his treks into the inner city to share the gospel with street people. He was honest and unpretentious, and that captivated me. He also had a great sense of humor.

I came to think of him as a model for a great priest. Somewhere inside me, I longed to know God the way he did. While I would talk about God as a mysterious figure, Mike would talk of God as if he was a friend. I think he was the first person who gave me a sense of Jesus as a person who could smile and of God finding humor in our world.

Mike loved life and in every respect was a real person. But these same attributes did not help him with seminary authorities. His lack of appreciation for seminary discipline often got him into trouble. While I didn't need any help from him, we often got into trouble together. After the grand silence, we would sometimes hide under the main altar and talk. We had to be very careful when the former Navy chaplain was on night duty. He had a large flashlight that he would beam back and forth on the wall of the chapel. I sometimes imagined myself in a prisoner-of-war camp. When we weren't caught, there was something delightful about being disobedient, but many times we were caught, and as a punishment we would have to pull weeds on the property or plant new shrubs at the bishop's residence.

One early evening I saw Michael standing with his suitcase by the door. He had been asked to leave the seminary, and in some ways it was a mutual decision. But it disturbed me. As I found him a model of a fine future priest, I wondered about myself. With Mike gone, I tried to conform to the image of a good seminarian.

Months later, Mike visited the seminary. His hair was cut very short. He had enlisted in the Marines, following in his father's footsteps, and was off to a place called Vietnam. He was also engaged, and I reasoned that God had great plans for Mike as a husband and father. He would use Mike in the world.

All my experiences with street people in Chicago had expanded my world, and now my world was closing in on me. I often thought about my family, although I had little contact with them. When I was lonely or frustrated, I would often go to a seminarian lounge that had a fully stocked bar. I found myself drinking frequently, since most of the priests did not frown on moderate social drinking.

That second year in the seminary, I felt Mike's loss. I would often look at the main altar and smile wistfully, thinking of the two of us hiding underneath it and talking.

God compensated by giving me a new spiritual director that year, Father Howland. He was different from Father Brown; he never would have struck a religious pose to make an impression on me. Father Howland was a portly, red-haired Irishman who spent weekends watching sports on TV with a six-pack of beer close at hand. He had a healthy sense of humor and limitations as to how seriously he was willing to take the seminary environment.

During our first encounter, he sat back in his easy chair as I said, "Father, I don't feel I am suffering enough."

I told him that I prayed and fasted and knelt for long periods of time but still did not feel great spiritual growth. I told him that I had prayed for suffering.

With that he gave me a quick glare.

Finally, I said, "Can you give me additional penance?"

He went on watching television; then he looked at me for the longest time. His eyebrows went up, his eyes seemed to open with amazement, and he exclaimed, "Are you *crazy?*"

I was taken aback. I had expected that such a request would please a spiritual director. He shut off the TV, leaned toward me and pointed his index finger sternly. "Don't *ever* go looking for suffering. Just live your life fully. It will find *you!*"

And that was it. He went back to sipping his beer. No sermonizing. That was largely his advice for the year.

Inwardly, I thought that he lacked spiritual depth. It was only later, after years of living, that I realized he was one of the finest spiritual directors I ever had.

Not knowing then how sound his advice was, I continued a program of self-imposed penance, sometimes sleeping on a tile floor in one of the classrooms. I was always waiting for a sign from God to move me in one direction or another. I'd imitate certain saints, but their personalities fit me like a wrong-sized glove.

At the same time, I was still concerned with social issues. One afternoon, while walking south from the seminary, I saw a large and imposing building. It was Stateville Prison. I could barely see the roofs of several buildings because of the height of the concrete wall that enclosed the complex. When I asked my classmates about the prison, most had little but passing curiosity. But my interest was piqued, just as it had been about the poverty and street people in the inner city.

I wrote to the warden and asked if he would lock me up for a week with the other prisoners. Knowing what I do today, I am glad he didn't comply with my request. But he did give me a personal tour. Stateville was a classic prison, run by the infamous warden Frank Pate. Al Capone had once been there, as well as other Italian gang members.

When I entered the large, circular prison house, I was overwhelmed by the sight of what appeared to be a human zoo. In 1966, on my tour, prisoners were forbidden even to look a visitor in the eye. Long after my visit, I continued to be intrigued about the prison and prisoners. I even speculated about being a prison chaplain when I was finally a priest.

But for now I was concentrating on becoming a priest—period. I was becoming quite scrupulous in matters of ritual and church law. I enjoyed all parts of the liturgy and would carry the cross in procession, wave the incense ball or serve the priest with the water and wine cruets. I looked with disdain at other seminarians who didn't fold their hands properly in prayer or had the wrong posture as acolytes. As part of seminary teaching we heard the words, "Many are called, but few are chosen" so often I came to believe that I was set apart for a high and noble cause. I thought priests were very powerful because they had the ultimate power to forgive sins or leave them unforgiven and thereby could bar someone from heaven.

Then one afternoon, I received a call from Mike Coleman's mother.

"He's dead," she said. He had died in Vietnam at age twenty.

I went to my room, locked the door and ran a movie projector to replay a film Mike and I had made together. I looked at his image on the screen with disbelief. That evening I went to all the old places where we had spent time together. I looked under the main altar and walked the paths we used to walk together. About midnight, I knocked on Father Howland's door because he had known and liked Michael. I heard his deep voice say, "Come in."

He was sitting in his easy chair, staring at the shut-off television set, several empty beer cans beside him. There was little to say.

For a while we drank together, and it was soon clear that he had a higher tolerance than I did. I felt the effects after three beers—which was good because it lowered my resistance to Father Howland's proposition. With a sardonic grin and the gleeful look of a child, he said, "I have an idea. Let's do something to Father Paul." We both knew that the dean had made Mike's life especially difficult. Anger mingled with grief fueled me. I agreed.

First we went to the seminary garage, where Father Howland selected some large wrenches and assorted tools. Then, after disconnecting the water, he completely dismantled a toilet. Together we carried it up a staircase and placed it in front of the dean's door. We then filled the toilet with water and placed in the bowl a bouquet of flowers from the sanctuary altar. We hastily penciled a Latin inscription on a piece of paper and attached it to the toilet. It read "Seat of Wisdom." I knew that more than anyone, Michael would have enjoyed the prank.

Father Paul never found out who did it.

It was almost a month before Mike's body—or, specifically, his upper torso, which was all they could find—was shipped back home. A letter he had written to a friend about ministry to street people became his funeral eulogy. Essentially, he told us to go to the poor and preach the gospel.

My goals for serving God were not as clear-cut as Mike's had been. In fact the way I went about reaching them was all wrong. I hoped to help my family get to heaven and perhaps to command the respect of my brother Anthony and my uncle Marty, who was my aunt Josephine's Russian-Jewish husband. Both Anthony and Uncle Marty were agnostics, if not atheists, and thought little of organized religion.

My second year in the seminary, I was invited to Aunt Josephine and Uncle Marty's house during Christmas break. At dinner one night, I was wearing my clerical attire and was asked to bless the food. I stood up and recited an unusually long Latin prayer, then gestured a blessing broadly. My uncle in particular was not impressed and spent the entire meal challenging one doctrine after another. I pretended not to be annoyed, but I was. Indeed, I would graduate from seminary knowing a lot about philosophy but not knowing how to offer others a God that they would want to know. I wouldn't even know how much I lacked.

That spring I completed my philosophy degree, and received my bachelors in music as well from Elmhurst, as a tribute to Sig. The next step was theological study leading toward ordination.

* * *

We were sent to seminaries in different parts of the country, and I was assigned to Immaculate Conception Monastery, which had a major seminary run by Benedictine monks in the northwest corner of Missouri. There I would be preparing mentally, physically and spiritually for a lifetime as a priest. I wondered what effect a monastery setting would have on me.

At my mother's request, my father and brothers drove me to the monastery, some five hundred miles away. We attached a small trailer to the car to carry my books, clothes and bike—everything I owned. I didn't know then that it would be the last time the four of us would be together.

During the trip we joked some, but there were also long periods of silence. Sometimes my brothers would say, "If you change your mind, there's no shame in coming home." Other times they'd ask, "Are you really sure you want to do this?"

Beyond that there was little conversation.

They decided to drive straight through, get me settled in and drive back home immediately, alternating the driving during the eleven-hour trip back.

It was about two o'clock in the morning when my father pulled onto the rough gravel lot of a combination filling station and small cafe. As I got out of the car, cranking my neck back, I looked at the most awesome sky I had ever seen. Perhaps the rural darkness of Missouri was always like this, but I had never seen so many stars before, and it pointed out so brilliantly God's tremendous majesty. I often think back to that sky.

Everyone else was eager to get into the cafe. Seated around the table, my brothers talked with my father about horse racing because they were working with him on a mail-order book he had just completed called *How to Win at Horse Racing.* Then my brothers discussed their various business concerns. I was rather quiet, still basking in the grandeur of that vast array of stars. I must have seemed a fool to them. I imagined they thought I was throwing my life away—my hope of having a family, a home, a career.

Admittedly, I was feeling apprehensive too, although I didn't intend to be a Benedictine monk. Even so, I thought it would be fine for a time to be in that atmosphere which would mean simplicity, few possessions and renouncing women. I thought I'd enjoy the rest from city life, shopping malls, movie theaters and television. My brothers would never understand that.

Joe once asked me, "Why don't you like women?"

I never told him that while at St. Charles Borromeo Seminary I had a close friendship with a married woman who was the principal of a local Catholic school. Our friendship started out to be very platonic—just some walks in the woods and seeing a few movies together—but it became more romantic when we began holding hands and forming a strong emotional attachment. When I realized where things were going, I terminated the relationship, but it affirmed for me that under the proper circumstances I would find that a relationship with a woman was natural and good.

I wish I could have been vulnerable with Joe when he posed that question. It would have done a lot to bridge the gap between us. But I thought my place in the family was to keep from confiding such things, to represent God by being perfect the way God was perfect.

The four of us drove through the night on hilly country roads until we reached 136 West and the small town of Stanberry at daybreak. The gas-station attendant told us the monastery was another twenty-five miles west. We drove over one last hill, and I caught my first glimpse of Conception Abbey, two immense Romanesque towers of dark brick jutting out from gently rolling corn fields. The town of Conception, Missouri, was made up of the monastery and six or seven private homes that stood near it.

The monastery really did seem to be in the middle of nowhere. It was a large facility, consisting of hundreds of acres of farmland which the Benedictine monks leased out to local farmers, reserving part for their own crops. There was an abbey, which was the monastery; the basilica, which was the church; and the dormitories for the theology students. The property also had several small lakes, a large apple orchard and large corn fields. I loved nature, so I couldn't wait to explore every foot of the grounds.

It took about an hour to bring my possessions into my assigned room. Then I gave each family member a hug, and as they drove off, I watched the car until I could only see the trail of dust kicking up from the country road. I felt very alone at that moment and sad to see them go.

I immediately entered the basilica. This calmed my spirit as nothing else could. It was an immense wooden structure built in the late 1890s by monks of the order of St. Benedict who had immigrated from the mother abbey in Engelberg, Switzerland, in 1873.

It was built in the form of a cross, with the sanctuary facing east and the main doors facing west, as tradition would have it. The roof was supported by large wooden pillars elaborately decorated with gold-leaf designs. High above my head were frescos representing the life of Christ. There were dark oak choir stalls, large wooden pews and a very creaky wooden floor that my knees would come to know well.

As I knelt in prayer that first day, the monks entered, singing a Gregorian chant as part of their afternoon prayer. The sounds of the monks singing and chanting, which echoed so beautifully, remains with me today. I would never grow tired of that sound.

And so my days began at the monastery. At sunrise a monk dressed in black robe and hood would tug the thick rope leading to one of the bells in the twin towers. The sound of the bells would mingle with the sounds of the awakening farm animals and birds. What a beautiful sound it was!

The first activity of the morning was to praise God. While it was still dark, the monks would quietly enter the basilica. They seemed to walk so lightly that even the wooden floors did not creak. They would kneel, then sit in their assigned choir stalls.

The theology students were invited to join them, and I did frequently. I remember the pale, pink light coming from high windows above the frescos and the several candles that were lit in the choir-stall area. The rest of the basilica was dark. Aging Abbot Anselm Coppersmith, his face serene and deeply lined, would sit in his elaborately carved wooden throne on the left side of the choir, and opposite him, the prior, Father Donald Grabner.

After the service in the basilica, I would go to breakfast. On the way I would pass a statue of St. Benedict and often read the motto underneath, "That God may be glorified in all things." That was my prayer too.

The monks returned to prayer throughout the day. At five o'clock in the afternoon we had mass together. It was always a solemn sight to see the cross bearer flanked by two candle bearers slowly process down the main aisle. Forty or more monks dressed in black garments and large hoods followed, then the deacon, subdeacon and white-garbed acolytes, and the last to enter, the celebrant with his ornate, colorful vestments.

As I advanced in my studies, I was often called on to be the master of ceremonies, especially on feast days. It meant memorizing what everyone else, each celebrant at the altar, was to do. Essentially, it was like being a choreographer. I would quietly whisper instructions to each participant, pointing at a prayer to read, telling him when to sit, when to kneel, when to bless. On the holy days, there were twenty or more people to coordinate around the altar. On many occasions, I was permitted to incense the bishop or a visiting cardinal with the thurible.

The lifestyle of the Benedictine monks permeated the lives of the theology students. We lived in their environment, knelt with them in prayer, could join their canonical hours as often as we wanted. The frightening world outside—with the turmoil of civil rights, unrest in the cities, and Vietnam—had now disappeared. Life at Immaculate Conception was like a long retreat in which we had the opportunity to encounter God in silence, in stillness and in simplicity, free of many worldly distractions. Yet through no fault of the monastery, the disciplined life fed into my love of ritual and legalism.

While I most enjoyed that part of monastic life that intertwined me with the monks—the prayer at the canonical hours, the time to walk and enjoy nature—I was at Immaculate Conception as a theology graduate student. During the mornings and part of the afternoons, I would take courses in such areas as moral theology, homiletics, the history of liturgy, the history of the Middle Ages, the incarnation and redemption, the history of dogma, and Christian antiquities. I studied the works of early fathers such as Augustine, the writings of mystics such as St. John of the Cross and, of course, the rule of St. Benedict. Although I didn't choose philosophy as a major, my exposure to Plato, Aristotle and other philosophers stretched my mind.

God blessed me with my first spiritual director there, Father Jerome Hanus, a man who many years later would become the abbot of the monastery and eventually a bishop. He was a scholar with his feet squarely on the ground, a brilliant professor with a large heart.

Sometimes he would give me spiritual advice in the form of poems. He shared practical advice about working hard at my studies and spiritual exercises. Embracing a strong work ethic, one year he had me combining spiritual exercises with such manual labor as picking apples in the orchard or cleaning the basilica.

Father Hanus was the first person to introduce me to one-on-one confession. I was used to the customary dark box and the voice through the screen. Instead he would usher me into a well-lit room, seat us in two chairs facing each other and talk in a personal way with me as I admitted my sins. He made the sacrament personal, and very meaningful. Sometimes he would offer mass in a small lounge where my fellow theologians and I would share communion as if we were a family sharing a meal.

But while I liked the informality of Father Hanus's approach to confession and communion, the world of ritual had become my world. I was emotionally married to it. I was excited by a sense of history, a sense that we were imitating ceremonies and gestures performed in the same way for centuries.

Loving the church rituals as I did, it was natural to want to dress the part. In my first year at Immaculate Conception, I had a growing collection of religious garments, including a black cape which I wore over my cassock and a large pectoral cross (a religious ornament most often worn by bishops) that I wore constantly, usually beneath my outergarments. Perhaps I wore the cross because I hoped someday to be a bishop myself. I had two medieval-styled, floor-length, white surplices which became saturated with the sweet smell of the ceremonial smoke. I have those garments today, and I can still smell the incense.

I had many private spots at the monastery. One was a secluded side altar in the basilica. Another was a fish pond in a small garden that an elderly monk, Brother Pascal, tended. My favorite place was walking the hills of the apple orchard, especially at dusk. I was always alone, the wind fluttering my long robes. By now I had taken up the characteristic posture of a monk, my hands clasped behind my back, my head lowered.

One evening stands out most. While walking in the orchard, I saw a magnificent purple and pink sky at the edge of the orchard, with large bolts of lightning flashing across the horizon. I watched the storm for nearly thirty minutes, and at its apex the bolts of lightning etched the sky in a large radius, spiking halfway around the horizon. It never occurred to me how unsafe it was to stand next to trees during a lightning storm. I was too mesmerized by the power, the magnificence and the beauty of the lightning display. Simultaneously, it made me feel small and insignificant, yet important because of God's love. I suppose it was theophany to me—God speaking through nature and signs.

Sometimes at sunrise I would get into a small, wooden boat and row out on one of the lakes. On the larger, Lake Placid, I would stop rowing in the middle and say my morning prayers as the boat gently rocked and drifted. Even though I was destined to become a diocesan priest, I now contemplated remaining at the monastery and becoming a monk. I didn't want to return to life as usual. The monks had meaningful work to do in local hospitals, schools, churches, even prisons, yet they also had this still retreat in which to commune with God.

Even today, in the busyness of my present church and suburban life, how often I have yearned for those private places.

Not far from the monastery was the Convent of Perpetual Adoration, in Clyde, Missouri, staffed by Benedictine nuns. They were very kind and gentle people. For many years the convent was a cloister, meaning that no one from the outside could see or talk to the sisters. But by the late 1960s, the sisters could talk to clerics and theology students. I became a special friend to many of them and was called on to speak to them frequently.

The convent had a unique museum. Their spiritual director in the 1920s, Lucas Etkin, had collected religious relics from around the world—so many relics that they had to use the former chapel as a museum to house them. The sisters believed every relic was authentic: vials of coagulated blood from various martyrs, bone fragments, complete skeletons, straw from the manger, a fragment of linen from the tablecloth of the Last Supper, even a small, white feather from the dove that descended at Christ's baptism.

Many of the seminarians, including myself, found aspects of the museum funny, but we would never let the nuns see us smile or laugh. We didn't want to mock their belief. I always wondered who at the time of each biblical event had thought to save all these items.

One day one of the nuns asked if I wanted to see Father Etkin's room, a simple room which the nuns kept constantly dusted, though just as it was on the day he died in an auto accident in the 1920s. It was rarely shown to any outsider. On one wall there was a large oil painting of Jesus praying in the Garden of Gethsemane. In front of the painting was an oriental rug with a velvet-cushioned kneeler. The nun called my attention to the rug. There was an intricate pattern, but nothing out of the ordinary.

"Look again," she said.

Then I saw some black spots—first just a few, then several, then hundreds of black spots all around the kneeler. Suddenly I realized it was blood.

She opened Etkin's closet door, and there hanging from hooks were several flagellators, sticks with strips of leather and tiny, spiked metal balls on the ends. Father Etkin would whip himself across the back as a form of penance and self-mortification.

He was, of course, from a very different age, and I have to admit I admired his devotion and self-discipline.

During my first year at the monastery, there was a person I wholeheartedly admired—for very different reasons. Because my mother was fond of ceramic statues, I began shipping several to her made at the abbey in a small ceramics studio. The first time I visited the studio, I met Brother Pascal, who made the statues in slip molds. Our relationship would be the brightest I would have at the monastery. Brother Pascal was eighty-six years of age, and he had a charming personality. He was short and had a round face, round spectacles and a shiny, bald head.

Sometimes we would talk for hours. He would give me encouragement and spiritual direction. In many ways he was the first truly contemplative monk I had met—not dower and grim, but cheerful and smiling. He always sat with his back facing the window, and the sunlight would bathe him as he talked. Death didn't frighten him. He told me that he looked forward to death as union with his Lord. When he died the following year, I had the honor of being named in his will, which meant I was to be informed of his death; he owned nothing to leave to anyone.

Brother Pascal's passion for the religious life had lasted him a lifetime. I was sure that was the way it was for everyone—once you actually took orders. Then one day, one of my Bible professors, Father Ignatius Hunt, was called to the Vatican and asked to recant something he had written. The process went on for many months, and one early morning, while we walked together, he told me that he was leaving the priesthood. I was shocked, but in my own heart, I knew that I would never leave, no matter what trials would come my way.

The end of my first full year at the monastery came, and I was recommended for tonsure, the ceremony in which I would be ordained a cleric. I would officially be a member of the clergy in the Roman Catholic Church and could wear the Roman collar.

While it was customary to have tonsure in the monastery basilica, I obtained permission to have it in the seminary chapel back home so my family could be present. It was scheduled for the day after Easter. I wouldn't actually be home for Easter, because I needed to participate in the basilica ceremonies, but I would leave early that afternoon.

I called home and asked my mother how my father and brothers were. She said everything was fine. I told my dad about the ordination, and he said he would be there. I thought it was fitting that Holy Week led to my officially becoming a cleric. I increased my prayers and fasting and used the week as a time of great reflection.

After midnight on Good Friday morning, I looked out my dormitory window at a severe lightning storm over the apple orchards. Contemplating Christ's crucifixion, I asked God to make me suffer more so I could understand the suffering of his Son. I stayed up all night, praying.

It was still dark outside when there was a knock at my door. Being awake and fully dressed, I promptly answered it and was told I had a phone call. In an office, I picked up the phone and heard my brother Anthony's calm voice say, "Dad died."

I was silent for a long time, not being able to absorb the message. I asked him what happened, but he told me he would give me the details when I got home.

Sometimes we spoke over each other. This was one of those

times. Finally, I told him I would be home Sunday as scheduled, but he said angrily, "You come home right now!" Once before, at Anthony's wedding, I had put what I felt the church wanted above what my family wanted. Anthony wouldn't let me do that this time.

While the seminarians were in the basilica for morning prayer, I walked outside in the pouring rain. Completely soaked, I sped into the small cemetery and knelt by the grave of Brother Pascal, asking him to intercede for me. I knew I needed strength and wisdom from God.

After I changed out of my dripping clothes and packed hastily, A. J. took me to the airport. Within hours a taxi brought me to Joseph's house, and there I tried to comfort my mother.

Soon Joseph told me we had to be making certain arrangements. Joseph, Anthony and I drove to my parents' home. It was very quiet. In the hall carpet, I traced the deep imprints the gurney's wheels made as it took my father from the bedroom to the ambulance. My father had had a massive heart attack in his sleep at about five o'clock that morning. He survived the trip to the hospital but died soon afterward in the emergency room.

When I followed the wheel tracks into the bedroom, the reality of my dad's death hit me. I saw my parents' unmade bed and his wristwatch on the night stand. Putting the watch to my ear, I heard its steady *tick, tick, tick.* How final is death. How ironic. Here was my father's watch keeping perfect time, yet my father's heart was no longer beating.

My brother removed my father's best suit from the closet, and we left for the funeral home. At the funeral home we looked at caskets and vaults costing thousands of dollars. Being the oldest, Joseph immediately took charge. He asked my opinion from time to time but basically made the decisions.

All the time I was thinking of the simplicity and dignity of the monastic funerals I'd attended. Those funerals had always impressed me, as they downplayed the person's mortal remains and concentrated on his spirit and life to come. Monks were buried in plain, handcrafted, wooden coffins, often made ahead of time by the persons who would one day use them, if they had the skills.

The unembalmed body was first laid out in the baptistry, beneath one of the huge towers. When it was time for burial, the coffin would be brought to the small cemetery on the property, and I will never forget seeing the simple pine coffin lowered with ropes into the hole. Then the dirt was hand shoveled, and I could sometimes hear the thin lid crack under the weight of the dirt. How different from the vacuum-sealed, steel casket we would purchase for my father!

I knew my brothers, especially Joseph, didn't understand how different a world I had just come from, so I kept my preference for simple funerals to myself.

The visitation began on Easter Sunday. When I entered the funeral parlor and saw a rosary intertwined among my father's fingers, I asked the funeral director to remove it, since my father had never prayed the rosary. He did as I requested, but when Joseph entered the room he looked at me angrily.

"Why did you do that?" he said.

As I began to explain that removing the rosary was in no way meant as a desecration, but rather more true to my father's life, Joe cut me off saying, "I don't understand you! I just don't understand you!"

Repeatedly, people who worked with my father told me how he talked about me and how he supported my being a priest and what I wanted to do with my life. I would never have guessed that he talked about me or was proud of me. In some ways it stunned me.

Why couldn't he say those things directly to me? I wondered.

In the older Italian tradition, my mother did not hold back emotion. She thought it was healthy, not only for her, but for her sons, to cry beside the casket and even speak to the body.

During the two full days of visitation, something was haunting me. No one knew what I was thinking because I didn't share it, but I was trying to remember one time—just one time in the twenty-two years of my life— that my father had said to me, "I love you."

I couldn't remember one instance and that pained me. I believe he loved me in his own way, but I couldn't remember one
time that he had ever said it. I tried to remember him touching
me, putting his arm around my shoulder, just any sign of physical
affection. I only knew of one photograph in which he was touching me, and in that I was a baby. I hadn't seen him for some time,
and when last I saw him, I couldn't remember if we even shook
hands. Even when he left me at the monastery, the hug that
passed between us had been something I'd initiated. I hadn't felt
any response from him.

Sometimes as I looked at his body I felt as though I were
looking at a stranger. I wanted so desperately to remember good
things and to have good memories. I remembered our annual
trips to the zoo, but they were long ago. Then I'd have images
of him screaming at a thoroughbred at the track, throwing an ash
tray or waving his gun. In my mind, I kept hearing him say,
"Horses!"—the response he'd given the doctor.

I began to cry.

Looking over at me, my mother and brothers were pleased. My
tears became sobs, which I could not control. My brother Anthony was sent to escort me to a side area where I could give vent
to my tears.

I was feeling a loss, but it was the sadness of lost opportunities
and the knowledge that I wouldn't have any more time in which
to hear him say just once, "I love you."

As was customary, the funeral service was held in a cemetery
chapel and no one went to the grave. When I told my mother I
would walk home from the cemetery, which was only a few
blocks from our house, my mother understood that I wanted
some moments alone with my father. However, Joe followed me
back to the chapel.

"What do you think you're doing?" he said, visibly upset.

I began to explain, and he interrupted me, saying, "You're odd!
How do you think this looks?"

He left me then. We both knew it would be impossible to
understand each other.

The funeral director was not obligated to remain with the coffin, but he decided to wait because I was waiting. It was noon and all the cemetery workers were breaking for lunch. The funeral director handed some of them five-dollar bills, hoping to coax them back from lunch early so I wouldn't have to wait long.

That next hour I made my peace with Dad. I walked behind the neat and carpeted chapel to where caskets were kept in a greenhouse. There I saw a dozen caskets lined up, each having a white sticker with a cemetery-plot number on it.

Despite the anger, hatred and confusion I felt growing up, something special happened in that greenhouse. I kept my hand on the bronze casket, and it struck me funny to see so many coffins waiting, as if in a traffic jam. My father was always so impatient with waiting, especially in traffic. I began strumming my fingers on the lid.

"I guess you have to wait now," I told him.

I realized I didn't hate him. I just wished that I had known him better. With his death, I felt a sense of relief, even freedom. It is hard even now to put that feeling into words. I felt I wouldn't have to worry anymore about grudges and fights.

A few cemetery workers came back, but because they were shorthanded, I was needed to help carry the casket. After it was lowered into the ground, I took a handful of dirt and threw it on. As I turned to leave, I noticed that just a few feet away from my father's grave was the grave of my friend Michael. I knew Michael was with the Lord, but I didn't know if my dad was. It was hard for me to entertain the notion that someone I loved and cared about could be lost. I had to cling to God's mercy.

The day after my father was buried, I had my tonsure. Dressed in a white alb and holding a candle, I marched down the aisle of the chapel for my ordination as a cleric. Several New York relatives were present, having stayed over from the funeral. When my name was read, I answered, *"Ad sum,"* in Latin ("I am here."). I knelt before the bishop who, using a pair of scissors, cut my hair in five places to symbolize the shape of a cross. I had committed myself to his authority, to that of the pope, and to the Holy Roman Church.

My mother cried during the ceremony—probably for losing my father and in a way losing me. There were other reasons for her tears as well. I found out later that Sammy, my father's friend who had been part of their mother's elopement, had visited the house and reminded her of the hurts of her marriage.

My mother explained many things about my father to me before I returned to the monastery. She confessed many things about their marriage.

"I loved him and I feared him," she said.

She explained some of the forces that made him who he was. His immigration to America, his growing up in the Brooklyn ghetto, the influences in his life. It helped me begin to understand him . . . much too late.

Less than a week before, when I'd called from the monastery, my mother had told me that everything was fine, but it wasn't true. I'd heard so many times growing up that she only stayed with my father because of us children. Now that the children were gone, she had finally made good on her claim. For the first time in her marriage, she had left my father a month before to live at my brother Anthony's house.

My mother had wanted to go to a party and my father, having a grudge against the person, had forbidden her. When my brother Anthony came to pick her up, my father and brother had had a fierce argument that escalated into a physical confrontation. My brother ended up pinning my father to the floor and then taking my mother home with him. Anthony later wrote my father an apology, but the letter arrived in the mail on Good Friday, after my father had died.

When my mother moved in with Anthony, my father would call frequently, saying he missed her desperately and begging her to return. She did return, but only several days before his death. Yet, she was never convinced anything would really have changed. Actually, she feared she would spend her last years penniless as he continued gambling. At the time of his death he was scheduled to go to the Kentucky Derby in several weeks and was planning to remortgage their house to move close to a racetrack in Florida.

Though I felt that things were resolved between my father and me, I became more and more introspective when I returned to the monastery. I would sometimes lock myself in my room for long periods. Some friends, trying to break me out of my sullen mood, asked me to try out for a play that the clerics were to perform for Catholic high schools in the Kansas City area.

A play done by a monastic community had to be all male and make statements about the faith. As a result, past plays included Dante's *Inferno, The Happy Jail Bird* and *Domitian.* This year, they selected *Luther,* by John Osborn, a play that had been on Broadway. They chose it because they believed the play was an indictment of the Reformation and a vindication of Pope Leo X. Through careful direction, Luther would be characterized as a brooding, overly scrupulous fanatic, a borderline psychotic.

I got a very good part, that of Cardinal Giacomo Cajetan, a representative of the pope in Germany who threatened Luther first with censure of his writings and teachings, next with suspension of his priestly powers, then with removal from his religious order and finally with excommunication.

Even during rehearsals, my character received applause. It never would have occurred to me that God would use my being in a play to prepare me for a dramatic event in real life.

Few costumes needed to be made for the play; religious garments hadn't changed much over the centuries. The abbot had obtained permission from the Cardinal of St. Louis to borrow a set of his robes. These were to be my costume. I was excited by this prospect, and when they arrived, I went to my room, locked the door and carefully removed the red cassock with matching sash and scarlet cape from the suit bag. Only the zuchetto for my head and the red-glass "ruby" ring were costumes.

Though each evening the play began at eight o'clock, I found myself putting the cardinal's robes on earlier and earlier. It only took about half an hour to fasten all the buttons, but by the last days of the performance, I was dressing by two o'clock in the afternoon, five hours before the beginning of the play. I would strut back and forth in front of a full-length mirror, and as I did, a feeling would come over me. I stood for the longest time looking at my reflection, and I liked what I saw. Looking back, though, I can see I wasn't just enveloping myself in robes, but in pride—the pride I thought I hated.

On stage, Cardinal Cajetan sat on our abbot's wooden throne from the chapter room. The cardinal didn't appear on stage until well into the play, but I would go backstage in a dark corner behind the ropes and sit in the ornate chair while I waited my cue. There I could imagine myself walking the marble halls of the Vatican underneath those majestic arches by Bernini.

In real life I had not earned even the title of *Father,* yet many people in the community, especially the elderly, would use the salutation, and I would accept it gratefully. I liked the idea of being set apart, even above other people. As I sat backstage, I told God that if ever I really became a cardinal, or even the pope, I would use power wisely and not be corrupted. But looking back I see that I was enveloped in pride. I loved the institution of the church without deeply loving God. I had no real interest in Scripture—just in canon law and traditions, pomp and ceremony. I depended on theophany, expecting God to privately reveal his will to me. Though I believed I took my promise back in Texarkana seriously, I wasn't willing to come to God in his way, on his terms.

I secretly hoped that I would someday be at the Vatican. I had a sense that I was holy—and not only because I was imitating my superiors. I simply didn't think I was a sinner; I felt confident that my works pleased God because of the penance, the sacrifices, the multiplication of visits to the basilica. I was sure God was pleased with me because I did so many good things and was willing to give up possessions and marriage.

Yet a patient and pursuing God was with me even as I became more and more like a Pharisee. And he had a plan for confronting me when I least expected it.

The Chicago apartment building Don's grandfather built in 1922 still stands today.

Family and friends of Don's grandparents gather in the basement for a lavish meal. Angelo Genna was a family friend (inset).

Don would slip into the balcony of this church on his way home from school.

Sig Swanson, Don's music teacher and mentor.

Don in clerical garments as he conducted the seminary choir (above). The main altar in the seminary chapel where Don and his friend Michael often hid (below).

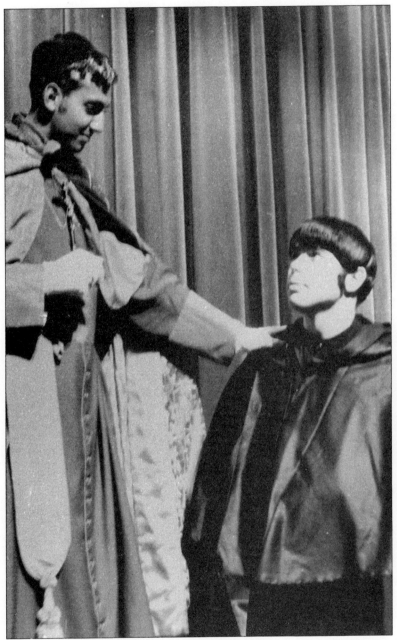

Dressed in the Cardinal's robes for the play Luther.

Posing with his film company in 1975 (above) and directing actress/singer Eartha Kitt for an NBC television special in 1976 (below).

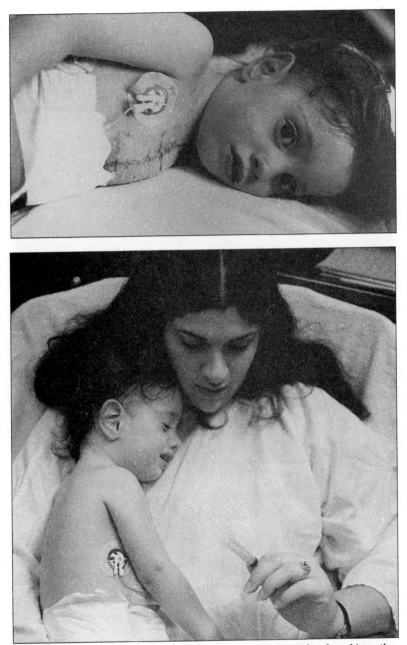

Luke after his second open-heart surgery (above). Receiving comfort from his mother, Gina (below).

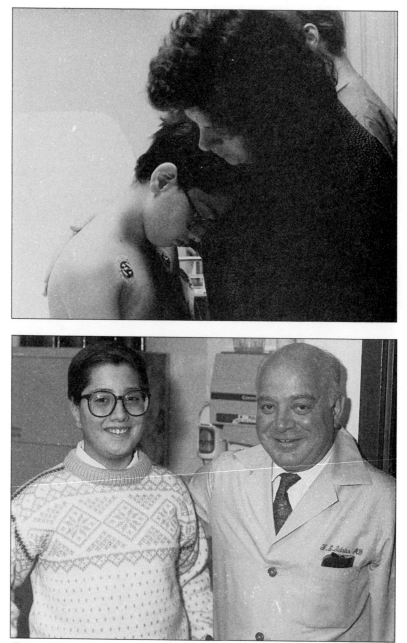

Gina and Luke after his third open-heart surgery (above). Luke is now taller than Dr. Idriss, his heart surgeon (below).

The witness stand where Don was forced to testify in his brother's trial (above). Surrounded by members of the Villa Lobos gang (below).

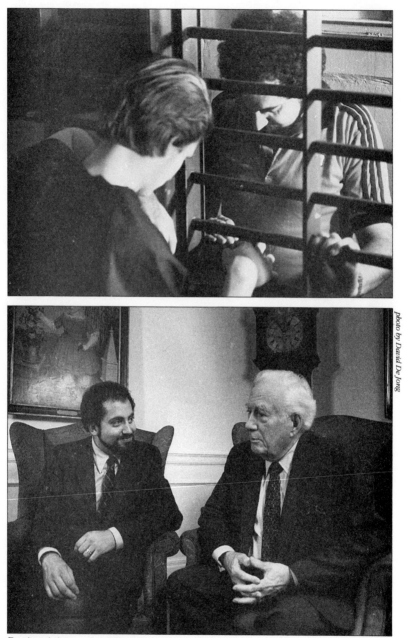

Don's ministry takes him into many prisons (above). Talking with Chief Justice Warren Burger at the Supreme Court (below).

Chapter 7

The Corn Field

THE TWENTY-FIVE-MILE RIDE TO THE SMALL, RURAL TOWN OF Stanberry was a Saturday-morning ritual for me and my closest classmates at the monastery. As I was sitting in Vern's car, I burst into laughter at the sight of A. J., my short, heavy, Italian classmate, wearing a pith helmet. Besides sharing my love of classical music and foreign films, he was always doing something to make me laugh.

All of us, A. J., Vern, Hugh, Tom and I, were from the same diocese back home. We were a support system to each other—a Saturday-morning social group as well as a solid study group tackling some of the more difficult theology courses.

These friends were important to me. We sometimes dreamed of the churches we would pastor ten and twenty years in the future. We knew we would continue to get together no matter how busy we got with parish life.

Everything seemed so clear and predictable and secure at this point in my life. My path was clear. My friendships were enriching. I enjoyed my ever-increasing role in the liturgy, especially as master of ceremonies. How I loved practicing ceremonial rubrics with precision, seeing people standing in just the right places, kneeling at the right times, reading the right words, doing everything as if it were good drama and choreography.

This Saturday morning, as usual, we drove east to Stanberry, a typical, rural Missouri town in which all the buildings formed a square. I always felt we added to the excitement of the place. It seemed as if everybody in bib overalls and baseball caps would stare at us from the moment we entered town.

There was only one restaurant, and the food wasn't very good, but it was a change of pace from the monastery's fare. Eating out, though, was pretty much the extent of our social life.

When we got back to the monastery in the early afternoon that day, I asked my friends if any of them wanted to drive the hundred miles to Kansas City to see a film. No one was available, so I decided I would go alone later that afternoon. I'd inherited a car from my father, and I enjoyed the independence it gave me.

As usual, I passed through the large, ornate basilica before returning to my room. I had a private spot where I enjoyed praying. It was a small side altar where I would kneel on the creaky, wooden steps.

That afternoon I knelt to pray as I had so many times before. But amid the reassuring predictability of that place, something strange stirred me as I knelt praying. While I had no desire to change, I wanted God to assure me that I was going in a direction he approved of. So using reverse logic, I told God I would keep doing everything as I had been unless he indicated otherwise by a significant sign.

In my heart, the word *significant* meant almost miraculous. I couldn't even imagine anything other than an apparition or the voice of God changing my direction.

Later that day, I obtained permission from my religious superior to drive to Kansas City, although I neglected to mention the film. I told him I would be visiting a religious bookstore and an ailing nun in a Benedictine convent.

Once I reached Kansas City, I fulfilled the letter of the law, visiting the nun and the bookstore for all of several minutes; then I went on to the theater.

I was quietly enjoying the film until a scene at the halfway point. The film was a satire of priests and nuns in Rome. They were wearing elaborate, if not garish, garments. In the film, an amused audience was mesmerized as the clerics strutted around in garments lit by flashing neon tubing and nuns roller-skated past wearing enormous Las Vegas-style headpieces. Then a bishop came on the stage in the movie. Dressed in a beautiful vestment studded with sparkling gems, he walked out slowly from behind a curtain. As he walked, however, a large gust of wind ripped open his vestment, revealing a rotted skeleton underneath.

In an instant, my mind said, *That's me.*

That's me? I immediately blocked out the thought. When *I* wore religious garments, it was not pretense! The film was no longer funny.

The camera moved in for a close-up of the spectators—cardboard cutouts with painted smiles.

When I walked back to my car, I thought of a passage in Matthew where Jesus was saying to the Pharisees, "You are like whitewashed tombs that look handsome on the outside but inside are full of dead men's bones."

"That's not me!" I said with the intensity with which Peter denied Christ.

I wasn't just unsettled for a moment. I sat in the car so long without starting the engine that the windshield became fogged from my breathing. I wanted to push the film images out of my mind, but it didn't work. I continued to feel as if somebody had hit me in the head with a two-by-four.

Movies are supposed to be entertaining. I kept reassuring myself. *The people on the screen were only actors, after all!*

I was real. But was the plot true of me?

Why couldn't I have seen a film closer to the monastery? The long ride back gave me too much time to think. Jesus' words to the Pharisees kept echoing in my mind.

For the first time, I wondered why Jesus had accused the religious leaders so heatedly if, in fact, they had tried so hard to live by the law. If such devout religious leaders could receive condemnation back then, was it possible that current religious leaders could be misdirected? Could *I* be?

I kept talking to myself and to God to try to make myself feel better. "Make this feeling go away," I said to God. "I am *not* a hypocrite. I am *not* an actor. I'm a *good person!*"

I kept thinking of all the good things I did, of the fasting and sacrifices and the long periods of kneeling. I reminded God that I followed the law to the letter and that I did it in his name. Yet, these thoughts didn't bring the consolation that they had in the past. When I'd sought refuge in legalism before, it had worked.

The long ride ended with one final hill before the majestic monastery came to view in the moonlight. Once inside, I started to walk up the stairs to my room, but suddenly stopped, turned around and walked outside instead, though it was already after midnight. I began walking east, soon leaving flat terrain and entering the cornstalks. The more I walked, the more restless I became.

Though a full moon had lit my drive back from Kansas City, the moon was now totally obscured. The night was completely dark—darker than I could imagine. I couldn't see my hand when I waved it even a few inches in front of me. From time to time I stumbled. Occasionally a large, dry leaf or stalk would hit me in the face, so I kept my arms in front of me, moving the brittle cornstalks to one side or the other.

My body mimicked the restlessness in my mind. My heart rate kept accelerating. My breathing became more rapid. Every step on brittle leaves seemed louder. Now I very much wanted a sign from God.

"Tell me I am doing the right thing," I asked. "Tell me that everything I do pleases you."

I desperately wanted that assurance. I had come too far in my clerical life to change direction so I didn't want to entertain the possibility that I was doing something wrong.

"Speak to me clearly!" I pleaded with God.

How I longed for a voice that would say, "I *am* pleased with you."

That's all I needed—a few short words from God, for then I could continue in peace. What I didn't want to admit was that such a statement would allow me to continue strutting around in religious garments, embracing legalism and feeling justified in all I did.

Misguided as it sounds today, I was actually writing God's lines for him. I wanted to play master of ceremonies—this time with God as the celebrant. At this point in my life, I had assumed that my thoughts were God's thoughts. I had no knowledge of a Scripture that said, "My thoughts are not your thoughts, neither are your ways my ways."

The security and peace that I usually felt were missing now in this lonely place. Again, I kept telling myself that I had come too far to change. I wanted God to tell me that everything was okay just as it was.

Finally, I stopped, slightly out of breath. Obviously, I had been walking in circles for nearly an hour. I was confused and alone.

Well, if God wasn't going to talk to me, then I would talk to him.

"I'm in this too deep," I told him. "Right or wrong, this is where I have got to stay. I'm doing all this in your name, so you *have* to be happy with me."

It was too quiet.

Though I was close to the monastery, I seemed hopelessly lost. I felt a mixture of humor and confusion.

If I keep making circles, I surmised, *I'll be in this corn field until sunrise.* By that point, I just wanted to go to sleep in my room and escape the doubts. Sleeping had worked at other times when I was troubled by loneliness or confusion. If only I could wake up in the morning feeling content and at peace!

"If you'll guide me out of this corn field, I'll deal with the questions another time."

While stopping to catch my breath, I heard a sound—faint but unquestionably real.

There shouldn't be any sound out here, I said to myself, feeling nervous and apprehensive.

I knew it wasn't my imagination, though for a second I wondered wildly if it were a UFO.

As I moved in the direction of the humming sound, one cautious step after another, the sound became slightly louder. I was very near it now, and when I extended my hand I touched a solid object. Immediately, I laughed in relief. My fingers easily identified weathered wood.

Of course! It's a telephone pole!

I was near the highway where there was a line of wooden telephone poles, some surrounded by cornstalks. Suddenly, to my amazement, I began to see the pole. It became light as the full moon emerged from behind the clouds that had hidden it. The light was reassuring. The world around me seemed almost bright once more. Now I could quickly find my way back to the monastery.

But as I tilted my head back to look at the moon, I saw the wooden T-bar that holds the phone and power lines at the top of the pole. The telephone pole formed a huge cross.

Thoughts of retreat vanished. In the roundabout, groping fashion that had typified my entire journey to God, I now had come to the most important moment of my spiritual life.

What was the meaning of the cross? Every part of my spirit seemed to plead for an answer.

In that moment God struck my heart like lightning. There were no visions, no burning bush, no voices, yet my Father in heaven was answering the prayer I'd prayed as a young high-school student in the balcony of the church, when I had asked so many times, "Who is the person on the cross?"

Now I knew, I really knew, that Christ had died for me. It was coupled with the more important revelation that I was a sinner, that I was *not* the good person I had thought I was a moment before. All at once I embraced the telephone pole and began to cry. I must have hugged that piece of wood for nearly an hour. I could imagine Jesus nailed to this pole, blood dripping from his wounds. I felt as if the blood were dripping over me, cleansing me of my sin and unworthiness.

How merciful God had been! How patient he had been, allowing me to take wrong turns, waiting as I became infatuated with an institution and with myself.

I have no doubt that the Holy Spirit used that telephone pole to save me. For the first time in my life, I knew that works would not get me to heaven and that my own merit could never make me good enough or acceptable before God. As I clung to that wooden pole, I realized how much I had loved myself, how I had used religious garments as costumes to imply I was more important than others and how I had hidden behind the laws of the church as a substitute for total exposure to God's Word.

I cried great tears of joy.

As I made my way back to the monastery in the bright moonlight, I felt the pectoral cross I was wearing under my clerical shirt. I took it out and looked at the faint image by moonlight. I had worn this cross day in and day out, yet I hadn't known the person the Corpus image represented.

I arrived in my room energized. I opened my Bible and began to read Romans, then Isaiah, then the four Gospels. Though I was already twenty-two and had studied the Scriptures as a theology student for over four years, I read the Bible that night as if for the very first time. I was experiencing the power of the Holy Spirit taking away blindness and deafness, and at last I understood things clearly.

As I look back, I can see there was certainly nothing supernatural about standing in the middle of a corn field late at night and touching a weatherworn telephone pole. That phone pole had been there for years, I imagine. And it would be there for years to come. But God had used it in my life, just the same. The experience was meant for me, personally, not anyone else. And it spoke to me in all its ordinariness. My life was never to be the same.

I waited until sunrise when the tolling of the bells called the monks to morning worship before I knocked on my friend Tom's door. With an excitement I'd never had before, I told him all about the movie, the anguish that followed, the corn field, the cross. He didn't understand. He was only the first.

My new understanding of who Jesus was and who he wanted to be in my life was so clear that I wasn't prepared for the blank looks and skepticism I received. Instead of sharing my joy, my classmates and superiors began thinking I was odd and strange. I felt a distance beginning to grow between us that I never thought possible.

What should I do with my experience? This became my most pressing question. I certainly had no thought of leaving the Roman Catholic Church; I wanted to become *more* involved—to help bring about change in the church.

Eventually, this conviction led me to meet with my bishop, an aging, pale, delicate man with white hair. He fingered his pectoral cross throughout our appointment, hardly ever looking right at me. He was a sincere and honest man, and I naively expected him to resonate with my news. I had but one main point: I must— we all must—put Jesus first and discard any doctrine that wasn't biblical. I still didn't know enough Reformation history to know I was treading on all-too-familiar ground and that I was headed straight for trouble.

The bishop was a man who had studied theology in the 1930s, growing up in the older ways and traditions; it was logical for him to command me to stop questioning official church teachings. And he did. At a subsequent meeting, the bishop told me to stop reading the Bible because it was leading me to interpretations that conflicted with the church. He explained patiently and carefully how I should allow my superiors to explain the meaning of the Bible and to submit to their authority. The new creature I was did not fit in well with his views.

A chasm grew between me and the institution I had grown up in. Now the religious ceremonies brought me no joy or consolation. Elaborate religious garments embarrassed me. I became impatient with sermons that were not centered on the Scriptures. I was restless during novenas or references to the intercession or worship of the Virgin Mary.

The monastery authorities began to view me with suspicion.

This painful situation lasted almost a year. Once a monk with a psychology degree referred me to see a psychologist in Kansas City. Because the man was an atheist, it was almost impossible to explain to him about a call from God. He quickly assumed I had auditory hallucinations. He'd say, "So you hear little voices? . . . Do you *see* God?"

Fortunately, a succession of interviews and a battery of tests demonstrated no pathology, which only made my authorities more frustrated.

But then my conflict was decided for me in a very odd, upsetting way. The rector invited me to a hastily drawn meeting. Many of the hooded monks in the room were my friends—people I had cared about deeply. But this day they were charging me with having a sexual relationship with a nun at the neighboring convent.

Listening to something so absurd first put me at ease. Sister Jean, a good friend at the Benedictine convent, was a sensitive, loving person who cared about me. In a brother-sister-like relationship, we would often walk the paths near the convent and share an interest in nature. Sister Jean would listen to my struggles and express the conflicts she too had had with her mother superior and how she ultimately had subjugated herself to her superior's views. This wonderful friendship that had grown for two years. It was pure and uncomplicated.

Knowing there was no truth in the charges that we were sexually involved and planned to marry, I was confident the monks could bring forth no witnesses or evidence to substantiate it. But I had momentarily forgotten that I did not live in a democratic atmosphere. I was not given evidence or the names of accusers. In fact, the trial, as it were, had taken place before I was invited to enter the room. I was simply given the verdict that I was guilty of the charges, and I was asked to leave the monastery.

God gave me a particular grace that day as the hearing ended. I was convinced that many of the monks did not believe the charges. Some could not look at me; instead they kept their eyes focused on the floor. A part of me was enraged, and yet God enabled me to stand up and go to each one of them and say, "I forgive you." And I meant it.

I know at least one of them knew what had happened that day. Tears were streaming down his cheeks.

I packed immediately. Then without so much as turning back to look at the twin towers, I drove off the property in the car. I loved the monastery and the people in it, but now I had been rejected. Though I had been contemplating joining the Benedictine order, obviously this door had been soundly closed, and I accepted the situation as God's permissive will, although it hurt me deeply.

Though I had intended to stay on the highway that would eventually take me home, I felt the urge to turn off as I approached the convent at Clyde. I suppose it was providential that Sister Jean opened the door. She looked at my sullen face and immediately expressed concern. I knew then that she knew nothing about what had happened. When I told her that I had been found guilty of having a sexual relationship with her, even of planning to marry her, she was speechless.

At that moment the mother superior entered the room. Sister Jean turned to her and told her what had happened. The mother superior was the birth sister of my monastery's prior. She said that she had given the information to the monastery. It all came together. Whatever the motives behind those who had created the rumor about Sister Jean and me, the mother superior had taken rumor as fact, bent on protecting the convent at any cost. I stood up and said that I needed to leave. I was hurt and shocked and angry.

Sister Jean burst into tears and fell to the ground, grabbing my ankle. I had to gently pull loose in order to leave.

I wouldn't see her again until many years later, when she was doing a residency at a Chicago hospital. Probably because she was not the troublemaker I was seen to be, she escaped my fate and wasn't asked to leave the convent. In the years to follow, she would become the mother superior of the Convent of Perpetual Adoration, proof in a way that no one seriously believed we'd been involved romantically. Despite the awful situation we'd been placed in, my memories of her are good ones.

As I drove home, away from the monastery and my life there, I realized I was still wearing my clerical garments and my Roman collar. I stopped at a small motel, and there a woman who I suppose was mentally ill came up to me, repeating the phrase, "Bless me, Father. Bless me, Father." I did bless her but no longer felt smug, believing I possessed some special power. Though I wasn't at the monastery, I was certain I would still become a priest. After all, there were many roads to the priesthood.

Back at my diocese, the bishop had me working with a priest who was starting a church in a new suburb, but after several months, my view that the Word of God was primary continued to put me at odds with certain church doctrines. At one point, I met with the bishop and part of his council. One of the key issues of the time was whether the seminarians prayed the rosary faithfully. When I went in to see the bishop, he asked if I prayed the rosary daily.

Before my confrontation with Jesus, I had prayed the rosary on occasion, but things had changed since then. I told him that I didn't pray the rosary, and this upset him.

One of my classmates was astonished when I told him what my answer had been.

"I don't either," he said, "but I told the old man what he wanted to hear." He chided me for not playing the game. I couldn't explain that I couldn't play those games anymore.

Eventually I was rejected by the diocese that I had tried to serve faithfully for nearly five years. The chancellor gave me the news in person. "This is the end of the line," he said abruptly.

In many ways, this rejection was a harder blow than leaving the monastery. Now I would never be a fellow worker with A. J., Vern, Hugh and Tom as the years went by. Since my trial at the monastery, I'd had to battle feelings that my support group hadn't been much of a support, because they never stepped forward to defend me. But I came to realize I still loved them and that their outcry probably wouldn't have helped anyway.

Father Kaffer, my former rector, did support me. When I phoned him after my dismissal, he gave me an illustration that I would carry with me even to today.

He said, "Sometimes God puts a wall in our path, and we must decide whether we are to stop, change direction or climb over the wall."

I took Father Kaffer's words as a charge. I still felt a call from God and was still determined that being a priest was the way to serve him. I was still a cleric.

For the next several years, I approached other major orders in an attempt to join other religious orders. In New York, I affiliated myself with a religious order for a six-month internship. But I didn't feel right about joining the order. Then I went to another diocese where a bishop accepted me. After a month of self-imposed retreat, I decided this new situation was not my place either.

I finally found a small religious order called the Scalabrinians. It had been created and was maintained by Italians. I lived with this religious order for a year and a half and loved those wonderful and warm people. The problem was that I was affirming the Word of God as fundamental. Being very conservative, and in some ways pre-Vatican II, they emphasized Mariology and traditions that I was moving away from. Though they wanted me to complete a three-month novitiate to join their order and then become a priest, I left them too.

There was still one more route that I thought God was asking me to try. In the history of Roman Catholicism, much good has come when individuals with different visions for the church have begun new religious orders. Francis of Assisi created the Franciscan order; Benedict created the Benedictine order; and so forth. I wasn't being pretentious. I simply thought God was leading me to start my own religious order within the Catholic Church, to focus on the primacy of God's Word and the centrality of Christ.

I visited a Jesuit priest who had once been my professor. He was well respected and had ties to the Vatican. He listened intently as I told him that I wanted to start my own religious order.

At one point, he laughed. His laughter hurt until I realized that it did not stem from mockery but political savvy.

He explained that starting a new order normally took years, that one had to demonstrate a substantial number of followers, and that in these days the creation of new orders was very rare.

I took his words as a challenge and sought out friends who had studied with me in the seminary and had also left. They were interested. One in particular, David, was willing to meet with me. Since he lived in Nebraska and I lived in Illinois, we decided to camp in Wisconsin and use the time as a retreat.

I excitedly shared my vision of the new religious order. Yet as we walked along a sandbar on the fourth day, he told me of his plans to marry a girl he had met recently. I knew that celibacy would be required of our order if it were to obtain church approval. I had mixed emotions over David's choice to marry. I was happy for him, but I felt let down. My dream of beginning my own religious order began to die that day.

I resisted leaving the church for many reasons. There was so much good within the Roman Church, I still see so much good there as I look back today: its use of the arts, symbols and architecture to represent the transcendental. I admired the parish system, the church's respect for tradition and its sense of sacred place in the sanctuary. In the monastery I had learned invaluable habits of meditation and contemplation, and the value of listening for God's voice. Yet when I did hear God's call to me, it seemed to take me away from many traditions I had held dear.

I was almost twenty-six when I finally made the difficult decision to leave the Roman Catholic Church. Part of me was haunted by the phrase, "There is no salvation outside of the Catholic Church," but I took the step anyway.

My overriding question became, "What do I do with my call from God?"

At first, I felt very alone. Moving back home with my mother was a dark time. My family's reactions compounded my depression. Joseph, I think, considered me unstable after he telephoned the monastery and talked to someone who said I was crazy. Even my more tolerant family members saw me as a failure, an embarrassment or a curiosity. I had to reconcile myself to the fact that at family gatherings for years to come, I would hear relatives whispering, "That was the one who was going to be a priest."

I desperately needed some reassurance that I was doing the right thing despite all the pain it was causing. I needed a place to fit in. But where does a former cleric go?

I pulled out of mothballs my skill in film-making—an avocation I'd begun with my father's home-movie camera the summer I'd roamed the streets of Chicago and had kept up during my seminary days by making a series of serious films. I began teaching film at a local community college and doing free-lance work with commercial filmmakers in Chicago. But I was from another world.

Despite the lack of confirmation around me, the experience in the corn field remained in my mind and my heart. I knew there was no turning back. That day kneeling in the basilica, I had asked God for a sign. The sign led me to a personal reformation. I came to realize how terribly wrong I had been about Luther and Calvin, and how I had glossed over the bad moments of Roman Catholic history.

The irony that I, "the priest," would be the first in my family to become a Protestant was compounded by the fact that the very statues my mother displayed in her bedroom, the devotions that many of my family members practiced, had come from me during my years as a cleric.

But I now knew that God's grace was a greater force than meeting anyone's expectations and was able even to overcome culture and family tradition.

Chapter 8

RETURN TO THE WORLD

I WAS WORKING AS AN ASSISTANT CAMERAMAN. IT WAS EXCITING to be working in film. While in college, I had been a crew member for an Emmy-award-winning director named Bud Churvas, and so when I found myself in need of secular work, I began my search in film. One of my first jobs back in the real world landed me in the middle of stacks of Encore Beer. Though I liked film-making, I didn't like much of what went with it—the drinking, the swearing, the high pressure. I knew, of course, that there are few occupations that let you escape from the daily grind of suburban life—traffic jams, crowded elevators—but I still longed for the slow-paced walks in the apple orchard of the monastery.

As a favor to an ad executive who had hired me for a few jobs, I agreed to do some volunteer work in an area high school. The school had been given a dozen super-8 movie cameras and for an hour each day for a semester, I would show the kids how to use the equipment and give them an overview of film-making.

When I first saw DuSable High School, I was surprised by what I saw. It looked more like a prison than a school, with most of its windows broken and boarded up. I parked in back of a car without tires or windshields. As I began walking toward the entrance of the school, three black students leaning out a second-story window began yelling, "Whitey! Whitey!" The chant was picked up by students sitting in other windows. I tried to fake a smile. A group of students blocked the doorway. I squeezed past them, only to find the door locked. Several laughed. I kept knocking until, through the small, screened window, I saw a woman security officer approaching.

Once I was through the door, I realized the atmosphere wasn't any more friendly inside. I almost stepped on a young girl who was writhing in pain on the floor. A girl holding her books said, "Someone kicked her in the stomach."

Even my class was antagonistic. The thirty students taking the course seemed to resent me. As far as I could tell, no one was listening to me, and there was no interaction. As the semester progressed, I was beginning to think I was wasting my time. Each day as I left the neighborhood, I would say, "God, what am I doing here?"

I had been involved in outreach ministry and counseling through the seminary, but my efforts then had been appreciated and I was able to share about spiritual things. It was hard to see the film class as ministry—let alone successful ministry.

One day someone started a fire in a locker near my classroom. When the building was evacuated, I decided I might as well go home. As I got into my car, a tall, black youth asked, "You're not coming back, are you?"

"What would make you say that?" I countered, though I knew he might be right.

"You don't really care about us," he said defiantly. "You go to your nice, clean suburbs every night. We go home to this." He gestured to the dilapidated buildings across the street.

I suppose I took his comment as a challenge. I kept going back, and to my great surprise, after a month, students began responding. The films they made were very good, and my world view was beginning to expand again. I think God used my semester at DuSable to prepare me for work with delinquent teens in years to come.

Meanwhile, within the next year I started my own independent film company. I began picking up jobs doing commercials and documentaries. Hardly anything made a profit at first, but I was growing in media skills and contacts. Over time, to make ends meet, I took an extra job at a Jesuit hospital, working in physical therapy with stroke patients and then in the clinical labs. God used that job to express his pursuing love.

One of my coworkers was always talking about the Lord. One day I asked her if she knew where I could find a Pentecostal church. I knew nothing about the charismatic movement; I was simply curious. Gloria Beyers thought my request was a joke. She belonged to a Pentecostal church, and she assumed I'd heard about her involvement there. When she realized I wasn't making fun of her, she invited me to come to an evening service.

Gloria was Italian, about forty-five and a wonderful, open person. She and her husband had two high-school children, a beautiful daughter and a son. Gloria's parents had immigrated from Italy and settled in a very Italian, very Catholic neighborhood. When Gloria was a child, her mother had broken away from the Catholic Church and become a member of a Bible church in the community—a radical move for an Italian in the 1940s.

The church had been founded by a man I knew and respected—Rev. John Marckese, a devout and godly man who was the first to encourage me when I came out of the Catholic Church, even giving me a key to his church so I could continue my habit of praying and fasting in secret.

The Bible church came under its share of attack. Some Italians would cross to the other side of the street so as not to pass in front of the church. Others only got close to the church so they could throw stones at it. But Gloria wasn't harmed by Italian hostility toward her church. She had grown up as a strong follower of Christ and married an equally strong Christian, Bill Beyers.

I had never known an Italian who had grown up as an evangelical. And when Gloria invited me home to meet her family that first night I attended her church, I knew I had never been exposed to a family like hers before. The Beyers opened their home to missionaries. Their children had grown up with a thorough grounding in Scripture and had been exposed to weekly Bible studies and prayer vigils. My own home experience was my only point of reference, and it was such a strong contrast to the Beyers's home. Here was an Italian family with a living relationship with Jesus Christ!

I really liked the whole family. Gloria's husband, Bill, had great integrity. Their son, John, showed an interest in my work. Not long after I got to know the family, he became my apprentice on some film projects. Their daughter, Regina, was very sweet and gentle.

I needed the haven the Beyers's family provided. Even though I was making friends and work contacts, I found the social transition back into the world very distressing. I had to keep reminding myself that I was no longer committed to celibacy; I was in my late twenties and didn't know where to begin with women. I dated several former nuns who taught at a local Catholic school. These relationships were largely unsuccessful. The former nuns were often as naive as I was. Our dates were either stimulating theological conversations or humorous physical encounters on a par with two thirteen-year-olds'. I'd think, *Should I kiss her? If so, when? For how long?*

It's no wonder my one date with a hospital receptionist bordered on frightening. After a day at a museum and dinner out, she invited me up to her apartment. She was obviously more liberal than I was, with her multitude of marijuana plants lining the window sill. Apparently she was more experienced than I was too, because without any preamble, she pushed me back onto her bed. I bounced back off and left soon after. As you might suspect, our relationship ended abruptly. In fact, every time she saw me coming down the hospital corridor, she laughed.

For a while, I kept to myself, eating alone and going to late-night movies. Living at home with my mother seemed more awkward than healing. She asked where I was going every time I left the house and where I had been when I came back. I realized later that she was making the wrong assumptions about what I was doing with my social time.

Sometimes after a late movie I'd go to an all-night restaurant, where I'd drink coffee and meditate by keeping a journal. Other evenings I would go to Melrose Park Bible Church. The pastor had given me a key so I could go there to pray as late and as long as I wished. Sometimes I'd pray for a few hours. Sometimes I'd pray till dawn.

My mother misinterpreted my late-night returns. She would often wake up if I came in at two in the morning and one night said, "I hope you are taking care of yourself."

Not knowing what she meant, I said, "Sure."

"You have to be careful," she insisted.

I thought she was talking about parking the car in bad neighborhoods.

Then she said, "You can get a disease, you know."

"What are you talking about?" I inquired.

Walking back to her bedroom, she murmured, "I know where single men go late at night."

I couldn't believe it! I was so angry, I hit the wall with my fist, which she reminded me was improper conduct for someone who had been studying to be a priest.

I began spending more time at the Beyers's house. Gloria's daughter, Gina, had graduated from a Christian high school and gone off to Evangel College in Springfield, Missouri. I continued to be a friend of the family, driving to their Wheaton home once or twice a week for dinner and church. I wrote Gina several fatherly letters, encouraging her to study hard and bringing her up to date on my filming activities.

Another family friend decided to drive down to Evangel to see Gina. I asked if I could go along, and he welcomed me. On the way down, Art told me how interested he was in Gina romantically. I suppose jealousy spurred me to take a second look. When I arrived at the college I realized that Gina had become a beautiful woman without my even realizing it.

A group of us went to see a movie, *The Way We Were*. When the movie was over, Gina and I trailed behind the rest of the group. In the parking lot of the movie theater we looked at each other for the longest time. That first kiss was so natural and so wonderful. I knew then and there I had no call to celibacy.

Though I was almost ten years older than Gina was, there seemed to be no true difference between us. Simply put, we loved each other. That's what was so wonderful and surprising! I soon discovered I was an incurable romantic who loved to send flowers and cards. I enjoyed making Gina happy.

Gina finished a year at Evangel College and then went to work at a hospital, administering cardiology tests. I was now teaching film at a local college. After we had known each other about two years, one evening I got on one knee and proposed . . . and without hesitating, Gina accepted.

During those happy years dating Gina, I was starting to make a lot of industry contacts, and my film career was taking off. I did a lucrative Air Canada commercial and then directed an NBC show with actress and singer Eartha Kitt. After that I directed a major film. An NBC television series profiling Chicago artists did a show on me and my films. John Banahan, the host, called me one of the finest underground filmmakers in Chicago. That year, a full-length feature film I directed premiered in a Chicago theater. Gene Siskel gave it a review. I also covered the '76 presidential campaign as a camera stringer for public broadcasting and traveled with President Ford in the Midwest. Things couldn't have been going better. As the American model goes, I was a success. Films were my future. I was still interested in ministry, but I would do it indirectly—through financial contributions. I could imagine myself in Hollywood someday.

Gina's and my wedding day was finally near. It would be a typical large, Italian wedding, similar to the one my mother always dreamed of—except it would be held in a Protestant church. The night before my wedding, my brothers Joseph and Anthony took me out for dinner. Something curious happened in the restaurant. Albert Jenner, a special prosecutor during the Watergate affair, was seated at a table nearby. Anthony sent him a bottle of wine with a hastily written note thanking him for his commitment to justice. Jenner returned the compliment by sending an expensive bottle of wine to our table.

My brother said he was impressed by Jenner's commitment to fight crime even at the highest levels. That scene was one I would find quite ironic years later, when I'd be pitted against this same brother over crime of a different kind.

The next day, Gina and I were married. My current motion-picture crew covered the wedding, filming from behind a stand of palm trees. But what made the wedding more memorable was the music that accompanied the communion service and recessional. We had inadvertently scheduled our wedding to take place at the same time that the Lombard Lilac Parade would pass in front of the church. Gina and I walked back down the aisle not to the strains of Handel but to a spirited drum-and-bugle corps.

It was a fitting beginning to our life together because in our years of marriage Gina and I would come to realize that humor would be essential in our relationship.

At the reception hall, my brother Anthony, who was the best man, raised a glass of wine and toasted our health and prosperity. Then the celebration began. Food, food and more food. The tarantella. The Grand March. That would be the last Italian festivity in which I would see all my family and extended family. Of course I didn't know this at the time.

Gina and I spent our first days together on a romantic honeymoon cruise in the West Indies. I felt God had blessed me with so much. Truly, a wonderful wife is the greatest of all these blessings!

One night several months later, I had an unusual dream. In the dream, I was walking in a large room with a shiny black floor. At one end of the room there was a bright, white light, and as I got closer, I saw a man clothed in a shining, white garment. He was standing over a baby bassinet. I looked at the baby and then asked the man in white, "Who is this child?"

He replied, "He is your son. His name is Luke."

The dream instantly awakened me from a sound sleep. I

remembered every detail clearly and shared them with Gina immediately. The whole experience left me with a wonderful feeling.

Gina and I were thinking about having a baby, but at the time of the dream, we didn't know Gina was pregnant. In June of 1977, we had a baby boy. I will never forget watching Luke's birth. Here I was, a man who had been committed to celibacy, experiencing firsthand how wonderful the birth of my own child could be. Sometime later, while Luke was resting quietly with his mother, I was awestruck by his tiny fingers and toes—so small yet so perfect.

This was the hospital Gina worked at, so the chief pediatrician did the physical examination and declared Luke perfectly healthy. Since Gina had been working in pediatric cardiology during her pregnancy, she wasn't concerned about "perfect health." Her prayer had been, "Just so the baby's *heart* is healthy. . . ."

I was so thankful to God for his blessings—and so ready to claim them—that I was totally unprepared when three months later I received Gina's call.

"We have an emergency!" she exclaimed.

My father-in-law had suffered a serious stroke the week before. I immediately worried that he had turned for the worse.

But she quickly continued, "Luke has to be rushed to the hospital."

I met them at Children's Memorial Hospital in Chicago. Gina and I soon learned that our baby was in chronic heart failure. Luke's persistent crying, which our pediatrician had said came from colic, was in fact a response to angina, or heart pain.

The next days were filled with doctors and waiting. After Luke received a cardiac catheterization to analyze his condition, we waited in his hospital room for news of the next step. Finally news arrived. A doctor said, quite unemotionally, "We have a very serious problem here."

I felt a sinking feeling. I kept thinking I was in a dream and this wasn't happening.

We learned that Luke's condition was complicated by a series of birth defects. It was called tetralogy of fallot. A substantial part of the wall dividing the two bottom heart chambers was missing. Also the pulmonary artery and aorta were connected, mixing blood with oxygen and blood without oxygen. There was also a narrowing of the artery that was creating high pressure in the heart, and the heart was enlarging to a dangerous size. Open-heart surgery was the only hope, but several doctors felt Luke was too young and too small to withstand open-heart surgery. They wanted to wait. After all, Luke's heart was only the size of his closed fist—as big as a walnut.

Other doctors, however, felt that if we waited any longer there would be irreversible damage to his lungs and heart. The line was straightforward. Without immediate medical intervention, he would die.

Joe had already called medical experts at other hospitals in Houston and at the Mayo Clinic. They had told us the pediatric heart surgeons at Children's were the best. Now the best were uncertain about how to proceed.

I didn't understand how God could be allowing this to happen. Those first three months with Luke were ones of inexplicable joy. Now I was so frightened that he would never come home again. I returned home one day to get extra clothes, and I walked into Luke's room. I looked at the baby crib, the little blue blanket and his stuffed toys, and I broke down crying. I pleaded with God to spare his life.

"Gina and I love you so much," I told God. "Please don't do this to us!"

The doctors were recommending that we agree to the high-risk surgery. I was reading library books on the topic, trying to make an informed decision. On one hand, within a matter of weeks we could lose Luke during surgery. Or, we could choose to bring him home and have him for several more months, but we would then surely lose him.

God's comfort and reassurance came to me in the form of my friend and pastor, Bob Harvey, at what is now Immanual Presbyterian Church in Wheaton. His was the first church in which I had become a member since leaving the Roman Catholic Church. He had nurtured me as a growing evangelical and had always taken time to talk and listen. The sight of him coming down the hospital corridor gave me peace. Many evenings we took walks around the hospital corridors. One evening in particular I asked him, "God knows how much this child means to us. Why would God take him away?"

Bob is a learned man who always speaks from the heart. The year before, the Lord had allowed Bob's teen-age daughter to die. In the simplest of terms, Bob kept assuring me that God knew what we felt and cared about us. God would never abandon us. As he told me God could use the difficult experiences in life, tears welled up in his eyes. His tears triggered my own. We stopped talking and simply hugged each other.

As the surgery date approached, I was overcome with uncertainty. I was hanging onto every thread of faith that I could, but I felt so doubtful and spiritually alone. One night I went downstairs to the small hospital chapel. Facing the marble shelf which served as an altar, there was a row of children's chairs. Luke might never get the chance to learn to sit up, to stand, to run. . . .

For days I'd been angry with God but hadn't admitted it. I felt that God was playing a cruel joke by giving me the joy of a son and then taking him away so soon.

It seemed especially unfair that this crisis had come on the heels of Bill Beyers's stroke. Gina's father was still very ill in another hospital, and Gina especially was commuting between the two. We were so very tired. We'd been lucky enough to get a room at the Ronald McDonald House—a guest house for parents of seriously ill hospital patients—but even that was exhausting in its own way. It was a world I had not known and didn't want to know. So many of our fellow guests had children who were dying, many of leukemia.

I felt as if I were becoming unraveled and didn't know how much more I could take.

These thoughts and emotions flooded me as I sat in the tiny chapel. I tried to pray but found that I couldn't. Then without much thought or deliberation, I walked up the small center aisle, took my closed fist and hit the altar with all my might.

But even in my lowest moments, I had to admit God had sent a messenger to care for me. Every time I turned around, Bob Harvey was there. He would usually sit in one corner of the room, quietly reading his Bible, always knowing when to speak and when to be silent. The hospital was almost fifty miles from Wheaton and sometimes Bob would come only for several minutes, saying he was "in the neighborhood." In later years, I couldn't remember details of Bob's sermons, but I would always remember Bob just being with us—representing Christ when we needed him most desperately.

Not everyone was as comforting as Bob. They all meant well, but some of their comments caused us pain. My mother would say, "What did we do that God would punish this child?"

I would have to fight the old thinking that suffering was necessary to earn God's approval. At that time, I had few fighting resources.

Once my oldest brother said, "Well, you're young. You can have other children."

Joseph's comment made me angry; I wasn't willing to give Luke up so easily. I in no way felt that one child could replace another. Whatever the cost, we were going to see this thing to the end and fight as hard as we could for the life of this child.

The night before surgery, Gina and I stayed in Luke's hospital room till well after midnight. Then we decided to return to the Ronald McDonald House, at least to shower and change clothes. Gina stopped off at the kitchen area on the second floor. I went ahead to the room.

When I walked in, the radio was on. That was odd, because we had never played the radio and had kept the automatic setting off. What was most surprising was that Luis Palau, an evangelist, was preaching about trust in God. I listened intently. At that moment Palau's message was just what I needed to hear. I was convinced God was using that message to build my trust. I woke up after just a few hours of sleep, and standing in the shower, I surrendered my child to God.

"I do trust you," I prayed. "You can have my child if that is your will."

The moment of release had finally come. I felt positive and refreshed.

It was still very dark as Gina and I walked arm in arm back to the hospital. Luke was sleeping like a little angel, and for a time I looked out the window at the physician's parking lot. There would be a total of three heart surgeons and nine other members on the team. As each car drove in, I wondered if that doctor had gotten enough sleep. I prayed that their hands would be perfectly steady and sure.

Preparations for surgery began. Luke was transferred to a surgical cart. But the most difficult part was saying good-by at the double doors leading to the corridor of the surgical rooms. As we each kissed our baby gently, Luke was fast asleep, holding on to his favorite teddy bear.

Gina and I sat with Bob Harvey in the parents' waiting room. The clock seemed to move so slowly. A nurse would come out of surgery periodically to give us reports. The first major report was that Luke was resting, which meant his heart had been stopped and Luke was on a machine. I tried not to think about the cutting and the spreading of the breastbone which I had read about in the medical books. I knew the surgeon would patch the holes between the chambers, shut off the shunt, put a contoured patch in the inside of the pulmonary artery. . . . It was all meticulous work.

Now the waiting room was nearly empty. My brother Anthony had joined us midway through the surgery. How I appreciated his presence! Luke had already been in surgery for eight hours, and there was no word. We were moving into an area of greater risk, as there was a possibility of lasting brain damage from Luke's being on the machine too long. After about nine hours, a nurse walked in and said that Luke's heart had been restarted and that the surgeon, Dr. Idriss, would be talking to us soon. After about ten hours, the double doors of the surgical corridor bolted open. We couldn't see our baby, for the cart was surrounded by doctors and nurses, one pushing a black air bag, two nurses holding poles with six IV bottles and other electronic apparatus.

We jolted from our seats when we saw Dr. Idriss standing in the doorway. He was a short, balding surgeon in his early fifties. His surgical cap and gown was completely wet from perspiration. He looked visibly tired as he said, "I believe it was a successful operation."

While he explained what could and could not be done in the amount of time they had to operate, my mind kept repeating the phrase, "Thank you, Jesus."

He added, "His heart was very small, you know. It was one of the most difficult surgeries I have performed." This from a surgeon with twenty years' experience.

Before Dr. Idriss concluded the short briefing, he said something that I will never forget: "I believe there was an angel in that operating room guiding my hand."

However he meant it, I have always taken his words at face value.

By the end of surgery, many friends had joined us in the waiting room. One friend, John who worked for InterVarsity, now led Luke's cheering section in a prayer of thanks. Oblivious to our surroundings, we formed our prayer circle in front of the entrance to the elevators, and blocked traffic for a moment or two. Then Gina and I went directly to Intensive Care.

The hospital had done a fine job in the briefing, but we were still not prepared for the sight we were to see. Luke's eyes were taped shut; his face was very puffy; he had a tube down his throat attached to the respirator for breathing. There were incisions for IV's, arterial lines and a large chest tube which was draining blood.

After watching Luke for almost half an hour, I fled to the restroom, no longer able to hold back tears. I got on my knees near the sink.

My tears violently expressed many, many emotions. Stress. Distress. Joy. One surgeon's warning before the operation came back to me: "It would be better if you would expect your child not to survive."

Well, we don't have to expect that now, I thought. Instead we could rejoice that at this point our child was alive. All the same, I knew I was near the edge emotionally. I really didn't think I could take anymore. Day by day was now hour by hour. Both Gina and I had to take everything in small increments. Tomorrow was just too much to contemplate.

On my next visit to Intensive Care, Bob Harvey went with me. I could see the amazement in his eyes when he looked at that small baby surrounded by apparatus. He remained speechless for some time afterward.

Gina and I spent the next week sleeping on couches right outside of Intensive Care, and we became friends with a couple who had a baby in kidney failure. One day we received news that their baby son had died. I will never forget what the mother told Gina. They were financially drained and could not afford to have the funeral home come to pick up their child and take him back to southern Indiana. They had decided they'd have to transport their baby in the trunk of their car.

We watched as they pulled out of the alley behind the Ronald McDonald House, heading home. Who at a tollbooth plaza or at a fast-food drive-in would suspect their grief? Who would even suspect that their child's body was in the trunk?

I still cannot explain the suffering of innocent children. It is a mystery that I will probably always live with, and one I hope will be illuminated in the kingdom to come.

Our baby was finally brought home, and a new, grinding stress replaced the stress of crisis. The aftercare at home all took its toll emotionally. My first task every morning was to go to Luke's room to see if he was breathing. He was on many medications which Gina needed to monitor carefully. There were frequent trips to the cardiologist and Luke's pediatrician.

Gina was bearing the majority of Luke's care. I was now working three jobs, including evenings and weekends, because our one insurance policy did not cover all the thousands upon thousands of dollars Luke had incurred. I was out of documentary film-making. The work was too speculative and too risky, considering our immediate needs.

At the time of my marriage, I had been at the height of commercial success. We had been blissfully happy. It had seemed as if it would continue like that forever. After Luke's surgery was successful, I believed again that the difficult days were behind us. I vaguely believed that there was a quota of suffering per person. Considering what we had been through, I felt certain that we'd already had our share. But new challenges to my faith did come only sixteen months after Luke's open-heart surgery.

After a year and a half, our toddler was looking like a machine that was running down. He would be playing and suddenly stop and lie on the floor for long intervals. As if part of a recurring nightmare, we were soon back at the hospital for another cardiac catheterization.

Now Luke was old enough to be confused and frightened by his circumstances. But he was still too young to understand the reasons for all the painful tests and procedures that happened to him. For the coronary arteriogram, Luke was strapped to a table surrounded by nurses, medical technicians and doctors in masks and gowns. I was allowed to enter for several minutes and tried to comfort Luke by diverting his attention, talking about his pet dog and goldfish.

It absolutely broke my heart when he said, "Daddy, take me home."

The words melted me, and I had to leave the room.

They made an incision in Luke's groin, opening the femoral artery and inserting a catheter which was threaded slowly up into his heart.

How I longed for a good report! At first the cardiologist reported a complication. His rubber glove had broken during the procedure, and they feared bacteria going to his heart, a condition known as endocarditis. Their first priority was treating that.

Then we heard the words we did not want to hear.

"We will need to do another open-heart surgery as soon as possible," he said flatly.

I swallowed hard and squeezed Gina's hand. We had hoped

they'd solved everything during the first surgery, but they reported a continuing heart enlargement, a high pressure in the
chamber because of narrowing in the pulmonary artery. And an
entirely new problem had surfaced: the pulmonic heart valve was
not functioning properly. Dr. Idriss, the chief heart surgeon, told
us he intended to remove Luke's own valve and replace it with
a porcine valve, the valve from a pig.

While we were waiting for a surgery date, one Friday afternoon
the film laboratory which was my primary employer told me my
job had been phased out. I was the third person to go in a month,
as they were trimming back, but I had counted on them keeping
me on at least through the period of surgery because of my need
for insurance.

The next day, unemployed, I took Luke to a park where he
played quietly. I remember saying to myself, "Don't lose hope.
. . . We'll get through this."

We were facing over one hundred thousand dollars in medical
bills without insurance, and that was a frightening prospect. I was
determined to do everything I could to help my family.

Yet God worked through others once again to bring about the
greatest help. The deacons of our church negotiated with the film
lab and picked up payments on a group policy, extending our
insurance for several months. This was an absolute godsend.

Even so, we were falling behind on our mortgage payments,
and my brother Anthony picked up two payments which amount-
ed to a thousand dollars. I was really moved by this gesture.

He said, "No one ever has to know. This is a gift, not a loan."

My in-laws were extremely generous. They gave us food and
clothing and money, often beyond their means.

Then Luke was back in the hospital as if he had never left. The
day of his open-heart surgery came. Again, the tearful good-by at
the entrance to the surgical corridor, and the all-too-familiar parents' waiting room. And there, standing beside us, was Bob Harvey.

This open-heart surgery lasted ten and one-half hours. When
Luke was finally in Intensive Care, we marveled that, compared

to last time, our son's body looked so large on the bed among all the familiar wires and tubes and apparatus. In the bed across from Luke was a young black boy who had received a trauma to his head. He was in a coma and his mother sat next to him, obviously in silent anguish.

Luke wasn't conscious for the first several days, but we made it a habit of speaking to him. On the second day, I was alone with him when a nurse rushed over.

"What did you do?" she said, sounding alarmed.

"I don't know what you mean," I responded, growing alarmed myself. I was afraid I had pulled out a cord or stepped on one of the wires going to the monitors.

Again, she queried, "What did you just do?"

"I was talking to him. That's all," I said. "I told him that his fish and his dog were waiting for him to come home, and that Mommy and Daddy loved him very much."

She said with amazement, "I was standing across the room, behind the nurses' station, looking at the monitors over your son's bed. Within thirty seconds, I saw his heart rate, his respiration and his blood pressure increase. Mr. Smarto," she said, nodding her head affirmatively, "he heard you and was responding inwardly."

That note of encouragement helped us through the days before Luke regained consciousness. In many ways, this recovery was more difficult than after the first surgery. There were complications, but we took each day as it came. Five weeks after his surgery, we brought Luke, in a brand-new sailor suit, home to his beloved fish and dog.

Chapter 9

ROCK BOTTOM

W"HEN IT RAINS, IT POURS."

It seemed that my mother's favorite saying was an apt description of my life. While Luke was still in the hospital, our basement partially flooded, and our car's engine burned out. Salvaging the contents of the basement was no small task for someone already exhausted, but it was a cinch next to buying even an economy car when we had no money for payments. To meet our financial obligations, I took as much work as I could get.

I let several local school systems know that I was available as a substitute teacher. This supplied me with a steady stream of work, but most of it was a far cry from my college major.

In a high school in an area called "the pit," I taught auto repair—ironic, since I'd recently ruined my car through lack of care. But the course work was less threatening than the students themselves. On one occasion a tool came flying over my head.

Often I was a P.E. teacher, struggling to coach players in a game I'd never played. It was really quite funny, but many times I was so preoccupied with survival that I couldn't see the humor in it.

The mental stress had taken a toll on my body. I had a nagging cough that wasn't improving. I avoided seeing the doctor, because I didn't have the money to pay his fee. I later discovered I had walking pneumonia and was hospitalized.

One particular day I did reach the limits of my endurance and patience. I was teaching in "the pit," several miles from home, and had borrowed my in-laws' car while my own was in the shop for repairs. After school, I walked to the car, exhausted. The students had really gotten on my nerves that day. The parking lot was nearly abandoned when I got there.

Then the car wouldn't start. I couldn't believe it! The starter had gone out. I sat there, hitting the steering wheel, saying, "God, why me?"

Up until then I had avoided getting a martyr complex, but now I was feeling singled out.

I began walking the four miles home, and on the way passed through into an affluent section of Wheaton with large, expensive homes. Somehow the struggles didn't seem fair. *I* was the educated one, but my brothers were the ones doing well financially. I was angry about the financial burdens and the need to work evenings and weekends.

I came to a pedestrian walkway under a busy street. I still remember standing in that dark, cold walkway because in that walkway I rebelled against God.

"Why can't you pick on somebody else!"

I immediately thought of how Theresa of Avila said suffering is a gift that God sends to his friends.

"Just be a little less friendly. I can't take your kind of friendship! I *dare* you to come stand in front of me. I promise I won't just tell you off—I'll punch you in the nose!"

There was no apparition, not even an angry God, and I was feeling terribly alone and abandoned. When I finally walked in the front door of my house, Gina looked at my face and immediately said, "What's the matter?"

Without thinking, I took my heavy briefcase and slammed it down as hard as I could, breaking a piece of the slate tile in the entryway. I wasn't angry at Gina; I was angry at God, but I couldn't get to him. I took my anger out on my surroundings. As Gina looked on, shocked, I broke a ceramic vase and then threw a shoe against a wall, making a dent in the wallboard.

Gina screamed at me, slapped me across the face and told me to get hold of myself. It worked. I sat on the edge of the bed and watched Luke crying from the fright I had given him. I was very ashamed of myself. In that moment I realized I had become like my father, doing the one thing I had promised I would never do in my entire life: have an uncontrolled temper tantrum and damage property.

Though I was coming apart, God's grace was still present and enabled me to do the right thing. After asking Gina's and Luke's forgiveness, I went to the phone and asked Pastor Harvey to come over to counsel me. He arrived promptly, and I was able to talk out some of my frustrations and feelings. In years past, I had put so much attention on looking holy. Now I was looking all too human, and I was wondering if I was growing in my faith or just sliding backward.

My attitude improved slightly but not my job situation. Substitute teaching became sporadic, and now with summer coming I started poring over the want ads for a more substantial job. One caught my attention: "World's largest photographic corporation looking for experienced men and women."

I got an interview. On a Saturday morning in a board room, I was surrounded by well-dressed regional directors and managers. I held back some of my professional credentials, especially as a cinematographer, so I wouldn't be overqualified.

The upper management flattered me with compliments and told me they were looking for a manager to open a new office in Amsterdam. What an answer to prayer! I'd been in Holland the year before making a documentary on the Netherlands, and I thought the country would be a wonderful place to live.

"I hope you understand," the regional director said, "that you need to start at the bottom."

It made good sense if I was to be a credible manager supervising photographers.

Gina and I rejoiced at what appeared to be an answer to prayer.

My in-laws shared our excitement. Since I had taught photography at a community college, I breezed through the basic training.

Photographic Corporation of America did family portraits in high-class department stores, but the new trainees began as child photographers in lesser stores. I was in for a surprise though. I soon discovered that starting at the bottom meant I was to go into department stores, hustling people to have their children photographed. There was one basic strategy: offer a photograph of the child for ninety-nine cents, but get the parents to pose with the child and hope they will buy thirty or forty dollars' worth of photographs when they return to pick up the ninety-nine-cent picture. It was probably one of the most difficult challenges of my life—and one of the toughest attacks on my ego.

I could barely get all the equipment in our small Chevette. Like a small photography studio, the complete rig included a carpet, backdrops, lights, a large camera, chairs, a table and a cash register. The equipment went all the way to the roof of the car and pushed my seat so far forward that the steering wheel brushed my chest as I drove to various locations.

My first assignment was a discount department store. I was required to make messages on the public address system, which I sometimes ended by saying, "Thank you for shopping at K-Mart." Problem was, I was at J. C. Penney. I had made thirty-seven documentaries and a feature-length film by this point in my life, and now I was talking baby talk, shaking rattles and waving fluffy toys to get babies to smile. As my skill at cheering babies increased, people would ask me if this were my career. It was all I could do to smile politely.

Every Monday, all the photographers would get together to turn in their receipts and participate in a motivational meeting. It had to be God's grace that got me through those meetings. I hadn't been making much money for the company, but others had. Every time people announced that they had gone over their quotas, a sales manager would ring a large bell and everyone would applaud. At one point in each meeting we all stood up and sang the corporate song. I couldn't believe they had a song!

After my stint in J. C. Penney, I was assigned to a Jupiter store in inner-city Chicago. I had never heard of this chain which did a brisk business in damaged and previously opened merchandise.

Feeling singled out for suffering, I now *expected* things to go wrong, and something did, in the form of a series of tremendous snowstorms which not only made my life miserable but lost Chicago's mayor, Michael Bilandic, the next election to Jane Byrne.

My sales manager insisted I go to the store even though the streets were barely passable. I ended up parking blocks from the store and dragging equipment through huge snowdrifts. The next morning I arrived early. As the store manager was turning the store lights on, I looked down at the carpet I had placed under my camera and saw a group of mice scurrying across it and under the counter. I just took a deep breath.

The next store was close to Austin and Grand, my old neighborhood. One afternoon while taking pictures, the snow started falling heavily. I decided to make sure my car wasn't stuck. It *was* stuck, of course. When I tried to move it to a better location, I lost control and went into a snowdrift.

I returned to the store only to find the front door locked and the lights out. I needed to get my camera and especially the money out of the cash register. I saw the manager, so I began rapping on the window. He recognized me but ignored me. I took my car keys and started hitting the glass as hard and as loudly as I could. By that point I didn't care if I broke the window. The manager merely shrugged his shoulders.

I exclaimed loudly, "My car is stuck!"

I could read his lips. "That's your problem," he responded.

When he left by the side door the other employees had used, I followed him to his car. He accused me of threatening him, but I hadn't. Though there was nothing I wanted to do more than to throw him into a snowdrift, I had decided to keep my hands to myself.

He drove off. The parking lot quickly emptied, and I found myself alone, wondering if I would die of exposure in a department-store parking lot. Every time I went out to Grand Avenue to flag down a taxi, a Chicago police car or a salt spreader, no vehicle even slowed down.

Two guys in a pickup truck eventually came by, and after I gave them ten dollars they succeeded in thoroughly submerging my car in the drift. It took several minutes of pounding my shoulder against the door just to get out of the car.

I finally got home but wanted to chew up that store manager. I did go back to get my equipment and give him a piece of my mind. He was an older man and didn't seem affected by what I said, but I told him I hoped that someday somebody would leave *him* stranded somewhere!

After nearly three months with the child-photography company, I quit one day, and rather abruptly. I brought all my equipment onto the loading dock and without so much as a good-by, drove off. A weekend at a Jewel Food Store on the south side of Chicago led to my unorthodox resignation.

The supermarket was in a high-crime area. As I carried the large cash register across the parking lot, I felt very uncomfortable. The manager brought me to the location where he wanted me to set up my equipment: the fruit section—oranges on one side and cucumbers on the other.

I managed to maintain my dignity until a certain couple began walking toward me. They were well dressed and spoke well when they said they wanted their picture taken, but I could smell alcohol on their breath. Then the man decided he didn't want to be in the picture after all, and the two of them started quarreling. Though I tried to keep the peace, their verbal fight became physical. The man pushed the woman into the oranges, breaking the frame on the display. Hundreds of oranges began rolling across my carpet and throughout the produce section. I held on to my camera, afraid it would crash to the floor at any moment. When security guards eventually came to remove the couple, I could only ask God, "Are you laughing at me?"

Two years before this I had had a Hollywood-style film premiere with large spotlights, tuxedos and a champagne party at the

Oakbrook Hilton; now I was a baby photographer in the fruit section of a store. The film equipment I had at home seemed to represent failure, a promising career that had dissolved. In some ways, I felt defeated and humiliated.

I decided to get back into filmmaking. I got an interview with a prominent director who was doing filming for television. I went to his studio with anticipation only to find he hadn't even opened the packet of sample scripts I had sent him. He said he would hire me, but I would start out by sweeping and mopping the sound-stage floor. My face and ears became red as the insult hit me. Reminding him of my past track record, I told him to keep his job. By this point I didn't know where to turn for dignified, paying work.

A good friend at our church, Bob Warburton, helped me get a part-time job teaching photography at College of DuPage, the community college for my county. I taught there for two years. At the same time, photography and video was expanding at the highly respected Christian college in my town, Wheaton College. I went there for a job interview.

When the personnel director told me there were no openings at the college, for some reason he suggested I look for work with the local county government. And even though I could only leave a résumé there, that step turned out to be a big one.

God sent me a big opportunity in the form of an envelope from the 18th Judicial Circuit Court of Illinois. I had a hard time opening the envelope. I was afraid I was being sued for not paying my bills. Instead, I found a letter from the Probation Department asking if I wanted to interview for a position as a juvenile probation officer. While I hadn't been a sociology major, some of the life experiences included on my résumé apparently had qualified me for the position.

Surprisingly, I got the job, and I accepted it, thinking I'd do it for several months while I looked for another media position. But what was even more surprising was that I soon found I had talents that matched the position and I really felt myself making a contribution to the juveniles and their families.

Though I enjoyed my job, the pay was minimal. It was hard not comparing my financial situation to my brothers', I have to admit, though. By most people's standards they were doing well! Anthony had a large beauty shop in an affluent suburb north of Chicago. Joseph was successful in sales and had bought a summer home in Wisconsin.

Their careers impressed the whole family—not just me. In contrast, with the exception of occasional requests to fix tickets or talk to a judge about a relative who had gotten into trouble, my work was largely ignored by the family. At one family dinner, Joseph and Anthony discussed the causes and solutions of juvenile delinquency without ever bringing me into the conversation. I felt like the Invisible Man.

Obviously, Joe and Anthony thought I was in an inferior line of work. They tried to steer me toward other occupations. At various times Joseph tried to convince me to sell insurance, recycled paper and cardboard boxes. I know he meant well, but I wished he could value what I actually was doing with my life.

By 1980, my brothers were not only doing well, as evidenced by new suits, cars, a summer home and extended travels, but they seemed to have a very private relationship that did not include me. At family gatherings I would walk into a room, and they would abruptly stop talking. Other times I would catch them glance at each other, stand up at the same time, put their coats on and leave.

Their wives and my mother would comment that the brothers were getting close, but the longer this behavior went on, the more it seemed odd to me. I once discovered they had met at a toll-way oasis. Their times together seemed more secretive than intimate.

One day Gina and I noticed how my brother Anthony's appearance had constantly changed. Within a period of several months, he went from a full beard and straight, parted hair to a short perm and a moustache; then he was clean-shaven and wore longer hair.

Anthony was becoming more and more of a mystery. I must admit, the first hint that I didn't have my brother's confidence had come soon after Gina and I had returned from our honeymoon. We learned that for all practical purposes Anthony and his wife had separated sometime before, even though they still came to family gatherings together in order to keep up appearances.

I found out about the separation when I stopped at his beauty shop one day. While he was busy with a customer, one of his workers asked me if Anthony was all right. Apparently, she and a few of the other employees were concerned about him.

She brought me to what previously had been the men's wash-room. When I opened the door, I saw a rocking chair, an end table with a lamp and a magazine rack all neatly positioned on a large, oval rug. There was a pipe resting in an ashtray on the table. Against one wall stood an army cot. Yet in every other way the small room was a restroom, complete with a urinal on the wall and a toilet in a metal stall. However, on the shelf over the rest-room sink were Anthony's comb, toothbrush, mouth wash and electric shaver.

"Your brother *lives* here," she said resoundingly.

Though that moment confirmed for me that my brothers and I lived in two different worlds, the gulf between us had done nothing but increase over the years.

And then Anthony began referring to himself as "The God-father" when the family was together. It started out as a joke, but the references continued. He seemed to be acting the role of a tycoon, while I was on the edge, struggling economically and still paying off hospital and doctors' bills from Luke's last surgery. Joe at the same time bought an expensive speedboat and was build-ing a new dock at his summer home.

One evening at a party, I noticed Anthony's youngest son look-ing at a large book of architectural drawings of homes worth well over half a million dollars.

"My dad's going to build us a new home," my nephew said.

Obviously, his beauty shop was very successful!

Success in business led to frequent travel. Anthony went to the major capitals of Europe, including London, Paris, Amsterdam, Berlin and Geneva. After several weeks in Russia, he returned home with a large, full beard and long hair, and made references to a romance with a Russian ballerina. I couldn't tell if it was fantasy or not. Several months later, Joseph and Anthony went to the Middle East. They told the family how they had ventured beyond a demilitarized zone and were stopped at gunpoint by the PLO. The family, especially the children, were amused by their adventures.

My brothers did ask me to travel with them and graciously offered to pay my way, but they didn't want wives along on their trips, and I wouldn't have left Gina behind.

In October of 1981, what started as an innocent phone call exposed the tip of an alarming iceberg. My mother had called to extend good wishes on my birthday. She added, "Your brother Tony would have called, but he's in California."

I knew that Anthony went to California frequently and asked her what he was doing.

She simply said, "Business."

When I asked what kind of business, she said defensively, "How would I know!"

I asked why somebody who owned a beauty shop went to California every couple of weeks. She became irritated.

"You're trying to put me on the spot," she said. "It's something I'm not supposed to talk about."

At that point, I realized there was something she knew, and perhaps other family members knew, that I didn't know. I was annoyed. My mother often accused me of not trying to be closer to my brothers, yet here was a classic example of them shutting me out of their lives.

"Is he selling drugs?" I questioned, hardly daring to ask.

My mother exploded, "How could you ever think such a thing of your brother? He would never do anything dishonest!"

She finally told me he was exploring the opportunity of opening a chain of tanning parlors and wanted to keep the assets away from his wife, who was divorcing him. I could tell she believed this story, but I had my doubts. Working in the criminal justice system, I had trained my mind to evaluate behavior and dig deeper. In this case, my digging was bringing me into places I didn't think I wanted to go.

Sometime after that phone call, in April of 1982, I received a substantial promotion in the court system with some very encouraging words from the chief judge. Several days later my family went to Anthony's home for a holiday dinner. After we ate, I saw Anthony look over to Joseph. Simultaneously they got up and went to the front-hall closet and put on their coats. Then Anthony turned to me and said, "Come, walk with us."

My mother immediately chimed in, "Yes, I like to see the brothers together."

It was cold outside, the sun had gone down, and a brisk wind stirred. I really didn't want to be walking outside. I was flanked on either side by my brothers. We had only walked about a block when Anthony began talking.

"You know we care about you," he said.

I nodded my head.

"We want you to get ahead. We know you've had a lot of bills the last couple of years. Joe and I have had some good luck in business recently, and we want to share it with you."

Joseph remained silent throughout the walk. Anthony continued, "I'd like to give you some money. You can open a small camera store, and we can go into business together."

I really appreciated the gesture but needed to let them know about my goals in the court system.

As I began to tell them of my recent promotion, Anthony interrupted me. "You know you're never going to get rich in that kind of work."

I added, "I'm also thinking about going to law school."

At that last comment, Joseph groaned, and Anthony responded, "Don't be a fool! Don't you understand what we're offering you? We're prepared to give you fifty thousand dollars right now if you will quit that work and come into business with us."

My mind reeled. *Fifty thousand dollars!*

I began shaking slightly from the chill of the wind, and the conversation had taken on a cold tone of its own, as both of them seemed angry with me. As we circled back toward the house, they assured me that the offer stood, and then Anthony added, "Let's keep this between us. We never had this conversation. Don't even tell Gina."

But on the drive home that night, I told Gina everything. Something didn't feel right.

Chapter 10

CORRECTIONAL WORK

THERE WAS NO SUCH THING AS A TYPICAL DAY FOR ME AS A JUVenile probational officer with over fifty clients. In fact, I can hardly imagine a more challenging job. Although the average age of the youth offenders was fifteen, their crimes were adult-sized: auto theft, assault and battery, armed robbery, arson and rape. The families often had as many problems as their children. Generally, the youths came from distressed, unemployed, low-income families, but I also had children of a police chief, a church pastor and several college professors.

People frequently pointed their fingers at the nearby Chicago justice system, citing graft and corruption, but I soon learned that the suburbs weren't so pristine. I would get an occasional bribe offer from a client, and once even from a county official. Since the only court I'd ever entered up till now was traffic court, I was experiencing a new world. But it wasn't new for long!

I was frequently on the witness stand. My duty as a court officer was to tell the truth. Afterwards, however, I often felt torn apart. Sometimes families would yell at me in the hallway, the prosecutor would accuse me of siding with the defense, and the defense would accuse me of siding with the prosecution. By making recommendations to the court I often walked a tightrope.

It was especially hard the first time my testimony against a juvenile resulted in his going to prison. I testified to violation of probation rules. In my opinion, we had run out of options. After the judge's pronouncement, the bailiff immediately put handcuffs on the fifteen-year-old and took him to a waiting police car. The mother was sobbing and accused me of hating her son. I knew he was headed for a dreary prison for teenagers where there would be gang intimidation and probably sexual abuse.

After the hearing, I went to the judge's chambers.

"Have you come for confession or absolution?" the Irish-Catholic judge said. Kevin Connolly wasn't the typical juvenile judge. A former prosecutor, he had a gruff exterior but was a sensitive and kind person. He liked the kids who came before him.

Many of the other judges who rotated into the juvenile division considered it a lowly assignment. Some prosecutors called it "lollypop court." It was a place where many young attorneys got their experience and then got out fast. Judge Connolly wasn't like that.

He asked me to sit down. I am sure he could tell I was upset; he too liked the boy who had been sent off to prison.

"If only I had set up more counseling sessions or tried one more program or had worked more with the family," I said mournfully.

His next words were important for me to hear.

"You are not responsible," he said, in the same deep tone he used in the courtroom. "You have to allow people freedom of choice. You gave him options. He didn't take them. He put himself in prison, not you. You must not take responsibility for people's failures, Don."

He was right. I felt a burden lift from my shoulders.

As I began walking toward the door, the judge cleared his throat to get my attention; "Oh, there's one more thing," he said. I turned, and he dramatically paused. "People also *get better* without us. If you don't take responsibility for their failures, don't take responsibility for their successes either."

I've tried to follow his advice ever since—especially with the success stories. I'm glad I can tell ex-offenders who straighten themselves out that they did the work, I didn't.

After two years in the juvenile division, I was moved to the adult division. One day I was standing outside the courtroom when one of my clients turned to me and said, "If the judge revokes my probation, I'll kill myself." He had suffered an emotional breakdown of sorts in Vietnam and was well on his way to becoming a permanent resident of the state's prisons. He had attempted suicide in the past, and what I was about to tell the judge would surely send him to prison. He originally had gotten probation after being convicted for incest, but then a series of nuisance and self-destructive crimes brought him back to court.

I took the witness stand and testified. The judge revoked his probation. He was sentenced to seven years in prison. He swore at me as he was taken out of the courtroom, handcuffed. The next day I received a call that he was found hanging by a bed sheet in his cell. Fortunately, he survived.

After I had worked with adults for over a year, the chief judge called me to his chambers. It frightened me at first because normally probation officers aren't singled out except when they're going to be reprimanded for something.

But instead he said, "In my thirteen years as a judge, you are the best probation officer I have ever met." To punctuate his statement, he slammed his closed fist on top of his desk.

I was so startled by his hitting the desk, I didn't actually hear what he said. "I beg your pardon," I responded.

"In my thirteen years as a judge, you are the best probation officer I have ever met! Why haven't you been promoted sooner?"

I was speechless.

He pointed out that there was an opening for assistant warden at the county's maximum-security detention facility, the second largest in the state and the most modern, with a capacity for sixty juveniles. He would recommend me for the job. It would mean a boost both in salary and responsibility.

I soon realized that his recommendation immediately put me

at odds with the patronage system within the facility. The warden had already decided to give the job to another employee. But a meeting of the full circuit judges soon confirmed me as the new assistant warden.

So I began a new job in "secure custody." The environment looked nonthreatening, but I soon learned there had been an escape attempted several years before when a teenager (who had murdered a young boy) put a knife to a worker's throat. Because the warden and I were the only people wearing complete sets of keys, we were the best targets for attack by someone wanting to escape. I could never let down my guard.

From the control-room window, the inmates looked like neighborhood children, but I got a different perspective. On my first day, I read the file of each juvenile. Two were there for murdering an elderly man by stabbing him over fifty times. Another, a straight-A student and the president of the local chapter of Christian Athletes, had repeatedly stabbed his teacher with an ice pick. Other offenses included attempted murder, arson, armed robbery, indecent liberties with a child, auto theft and burglary.

Each crime was enough to land a teen behind thick metal doors. In the three years I served in that institution I became accustomed to the loud slamming of those thick metal doors. I would have to go through as many as eight doors to get to some parts of the building, and they all slammed loud and hard.

Since some of the staff disapproved of my presence because they felt I'd been forced on them, they had a prank prepared for me on my first day. There was a fifteen-year-old girl screaming in her cell. A staff member asked if I would talk with her. She had been involved in prostitution since age twelve, yet her freckles and broad smile made her look like a Girl Scout. I was smart enough not to go into her cell alone, but I stood in the doorway, after unlocking it. As I looked into her cell, she quickly unzipped her jacket, revealing her naked breasts. Some amused staff watched my reaction from the control room.

Several months later a judge signed an order of transportation for me to drive the same girl a hundred miles to interview at a residential treatment center. I brought along Marsha, a very competent probation officer. During the appointment, the girl ran off across the street. Marsha and I chased her on foot, but I lost sight of her as she headed for a gas station.

I soon learned the limits of authority. When I showed the gas-station attendant my large, gold badge, he pretended he had never seen her. On closer inspection, we found her hiding in a closet. By the time we got her into my car, Marsha and I were heavily out of breath. The girl seemed to be doing fine.

On the way home, I was driving about seventy miles an hour on Interstate 90 when the girl, who was in the back seat with Marsha, reached over the driver's seat without warning and grabbed the steering wheel. We swerved two lanes to the right and then one lane to the left. I thanked God that there was no traffic on either side or there would have been a terrible accident. Marsha reached forward quickly and gave her a blow to the neck, which pacified her for the rest of the trip.

Arrested juveniles were brought to our facility at any hour of the day or night, and I would often go there to meet them. Even if innocent, a young boy or girl brought to the facility on a Friday evening would not be released until Monday morning. By policy, new arrests were isolated for the first twenty-four hours, a time when they were often despondent and crying. Their cell was small, with a thick metal door, a concrete slab with a thin mattress and a seatless toilet.

I was particularly disturbed when mentally ill juveniles were put in my facility. We simply weren't equipped to manage them. A young man named Jim stands out in my mind. He had auditory hallucinations. One day he smeared food and excrement all over the walls. I went into his room, sat down at a distance and carefully moved toward him inch by inch until he calmed down. I came out of his cell realizing that he thought he was living in a totally different state and time.

A juvenile's size never limited his or her capacity for violence when drugs were involved. One fifteen-year-old was temporarily locked in an interview room while a staff member went to pull a file. The staff member hadn't known that the young boy was high on acid. Within minutes, he demolished the room. I arrived to find blood and jagged glass on the floor and the table torn out of the wall and fluorescent tubes ripped out of the ceiling fixture. He'd used the jagged tubes to stab himself and intimidate the staff member.

The sight of what drugs were doing to youth prompted Judge Connolly and me to have a series of meetings. A recovering alcoholic, Judge Connolly had great empathy for troubled youth on drugs. He authorized me to study the feasibility of setting up our own residential drug-treatment program. A fine professional, Anne Fischer, and I began observing other drug programs.

A year later I was wearing two hats: assistant warden and director of a residential drug and alcohol program. The new program filled one wing of the building. Sixty-eight drug-abusing juveniles went through the program in its first year. NBC television did a program on us which called our program one of the most unique drug programs in the country.

Since it was a residential program which demanded total abstinence, the teens would often fall prey to the Mardi Gras Syndrome before entering the program. Just as some people live it up in the last days before Lent, these teens would ingest double or triple their usual dosage of alcohol, pot or cocaine to compensate for the lean times ahead. As a result, their first couple of days in treatment were racked by severe headaches, stomach cramps, nausea and dizziness. This initial phase always was hard on the staff.

One evening, just before I was about to give a talk to the parents of our residents, I was helping a young man who had a loss of motor control down a hallway. During our walk he vomited all over my suit. It was wonderful after two weeks to see the same youth clear-eyed, clear-minded and smiling, perhaps for the first time in years.

Many years later, I was in a department store at Christmas time. A young man came up to me and said hello. I didn't recognize him. He introduced me to his wife, showed me a picture of his two children and emphasized that he had been clean of drugs for several years. I finally realized he was the same young man who had vomited on my suit years before. The rewards for working with offenders or drug-dependent youth could be great indeed, but they were rarely immediate.

At this point, I expected to stay in correctional work for the rest of my professional life. I had taken the promotions as a sign from God that this is where I belonged. The warden was thinking of taking an early retirement, and I expected that I would fill his position. But I would soon discover that following Christ could cause some of my problems.

With a large staff working three shifts, it was inevitable that some employees had views far different from my own. One person disciplined juveniles by putting their heads in the toilet bowl and repeatedly flushing it. Some staff just stood back and allowed residents to abuse each other, such as by initiating a new resident by pinning him to the shower-room floor, spreading Ben-Gay ointment on his genitals and then pouring a bucket of ice over him. Some of the night shift resented me coming into the building after midnight, because they liked to relax the rules at night. Occasionally, I would find someone sleeping on a mattress behind the control room, a particular hazard if the building had to be evacuated in a fire. When such things happened and I found out about them, there would be conflict.

It all came to a head one Friday afternoon. As part of the drug program, I had brought in several college interns from several institutions, including Wheaton College. We would debrief and talk out problems each week in a confidential meeting room in the building where lawyers, psychologists and clergy could talk to the inmates.

One particular Friday afternoon, we were very startled when a staff member suddenly burst into the room and told us he resented being talked about. It took a few moments for reality to register. The room was bugged! I found two hidden microphones in the ceiling. I followed the wire in the attic to the control room where there was a capacity not only to monitor but to tape-record.

The college students were very upset, realizing that private conversations about their families and their schools may have been listened to, but I soon realized the deeper implications. If word ever got out that the confidentiality of the client-attorney relationship was violated in our facility, it could jeopardize and overturn cases.

Question upon question rushed through my head. *Had any conversations been tape-recorded? Over how long a period? Had any information during a trial been passed on to the prosecutor's office?*

My worst fears were realized when the staff member began to boast that he'd been listening to such conversations for a long time and felt it was helpful in working with the juveniles.

My immediate goal was the removal of the hidden microphones. I had assumed the warden did not know of their presence, until he told me to forget the whole matter. It was at that point that I went to my private attorney. He recommended a court injunction so the activity could be stopped.

Then an intern's faculty advisor leaked the story to Chicago's largest newspaper, the *Tribune*. Four days later, it appeared as a feature article. The head of the county probation department, the warden's boss, assumed I had blown the whistle.

Friends told me not to worry. "They can't hurt you for telling the truth."

My attorney said, "Don't worry. They can't fire you."

But I soon learned there are many ways within the system that people can use to make your life difficult besides dismissal.

The department head called me, furious. I think he was just as startled as I was by the practice but wanted to put a lid on the affair. While blowing cigarette smoke in my direction, he said, "You're dead in the water." He said my career in the criminal justice system had just come to an end.

I assumed I would never be in a courtroom again. I had worked diligently to build this career, and now I saw it falling apart before my eyes.

Soon my superiors found clever ways to eliminate the parts of my job I enjoyed the most. I had been in charge of the facility's public relations, including public speaking and giving tours. Now they hastily created a resource division that never requested my services as a spokesman. Soon I was no longer working with college interns, and the drug program was sabotaged. The other administrators avoided and shunned me, even calling meetings without me.

I wasn't totally ignorant of how the game was played politically. I knew standing up for a principle could bring tons of trouble my way, even if it helped the situation. And that's what happened.

I believe the warden's main goal was to get me out of the facility. He thought that attacking my pride would be the most successful route. But God gave me a strength, a perseverance and a patience in that situation I had never known before.

One day the warden informed me that my new major duty was cleaning the building's toilets, using the three-man maintenance staff. Rather than let this defeat me, I took it as a challenge. I came up with a chart and a graph. I experimented with different chemicals on the porcelain and stainless steel. I wanted this facility to have the shiniest, cleanest toilets anywhere. I really began to enjoy the task. The administrators were frustrated by my response, I could tell, but to my surprise, they didn't berate me.

And then something marvelous began happening. Another mindless task I'd been given was to go to the outside yard every morning at ten o'clock, before the juveniles came out for recreation. My big job was to kick the fence, make sure it hadn't been cut and look to see if anything had been thrown over the security fence. I used that twenty minutes a day as rich prayer time.

Unlike other times in my life, although I was frustrated, I felt neither anger nor defeat. I really believed God was going to do something powerful. Although my future didn't look hopeful at the correctional facility, I remained. The situation stayed bad for many months.

Then a glimmer of hope came in the form of a phone call from an organization called Prison Fellowship, a highly respected prison ministry with 200 staff and about 30,000 volunteers who work to enable the church to help prisoners and ex-prisoners in the community. The organization wanted me to fly to their Washington headquarters to interview for a job as the state director for Illinois. I met with most of the top management and by the end of the day was offered the job. I told them I needed some time to think about it, but flying back that same night, I was invigorated.

The next morning when I arrived at the correctional facility, I looked very confident. Then later that day I received a letter from Wheaton College saying I'd been suggested as a candidate for the director of the new Institute for Prison Ministries at the Billy Graham Center. I decided to apply for that job too.

I didn't think my final interview with the new Billy Graham Center director, Dr. James Kraakevik, went particularly well. On the way out of the building, I stopped in the museum chapel. While I rested there in God's presence, I realized my life had been a long journey with lots of turns; I put this next turn in the Lord's hands.

The day I was to hear from the college came and went. Then one day I was in Lake County giving a conference talk—a rare treat for me those days. While I was standing in the hotel lobby, I heard my name paged. I went to the front desk and picked up the phone. The warden of my facility and the department director were standing at my shoulder. In their presence, I heard the words, "The director's job is yours if you want it. Do you want the job?"

It didn't take me long to say yes. Immediately afterward, I went out to the parking lot where I began to cry tears of joy. God in his grace had helped me to be faithful during the ordeal, and he had not abandoned me.

That next Monday morning I entered the stately Billy Graham Center as director of the Institute for Prison Ministries. Since the center didn't have an office for me yet, they gave me Billy Graham's office, a ceremonial office which he used when on campus. I sat at his semi-circular desk among pictures of his Montreat home and his books, and I praised God. I had gone from an inspector of toilets to an administrator of an international program.

I remembered how disappointed I'd been when I wasn't hired at Wheaton some years before, yet through a referral by Wheaton's personnel director, Trig Larsen, I'd acquired the knowledge and experiences I needed in a whole new field which enabled me to come back and take the helm of this new program.

During my first year, I crisscrossed America, visiting more than fifty prisons and working with fine people like Bill Glass, a former pro-football player who for the last twenty years has been a full-time evangelist, and Chuck Colson, the founder of Prison Fellowship. Soon I was called back as a consultant to the training office of the Illinois Supreme Court to train probation officers. Next, the State Attorney's Office asked me to be a consultant for their drug-abuse task force. I once thought my ministry potential would never be used. Now I had unlimited opportunities to help heal the physical, social, emotional and spiritual wounds of prisoners.

My godly boss, Jim Kraakevik, warned me that I would be on the front lines of spiritual battle.

"Don't be surprised if you are assaulted," he said.

I never thought the threat would come from within my own family.

Chapter 11

ANTHONY'S ARREST

O NE OF THE MOST DRAMATIC PARTS OF MY LIFE BEGAN WHILE I was still working for the juvenile institution, but it didn't end until I was at the Graham Center. And, in some ways, it still hasn't ended.

One Saturday morning in September of 1982, I got a phone call from my brother Joseph asking me to hurry to his home.

"I'll explain when you get here," he said and then added, "This may be the most important conversation we will ever have."

I did hurry to his home, worried that one of our family was critically ill or dead and that Joe didn't want to break it to me over the phone. When I got there, he and his wife ushered me into the den. Though I must have seemed anxious to know what was up, they chatted initially about the weather and other matters.

Finally Joseph said, "Our brother, Tony, was arrested several days ago for trespassing in a bank."

Anthony arrested? I thought. Joe's wife shook her head in disbelief.

"We don't know why he was there," Joseph continued, "but he was taken to Lake County Jail and then bonded out. All I know is that he's in trouble and we need to help him. He needs his family to support him."

Joseph's wife went into the kitchen to make coffee. When she left, he leaned toward me and said, "Do you remember that walk we had outside some time ago?"

I couldn't recall.

He continued, "We wanted to help you out and offered you that fifty thousand dollars."

"Yes," I replied.

"Well, you can see how that could look now. The FBI is trying to pin all sorts of unsolved cases on Tony, and it could look bad. Remember," he said dramatically, "family comes before anything. We never had that conversation."

He asked me if I could think of any other ways I could help Anthony.

I said that if, in fact, Anthony was having some kind of a mental problem, I could suggest a good psychiatrist. Joseph reached for the telephone and called Anthony.

"Your brother Donnie is sitting here with me. He wants to help you. Talk to him." He handed the phone over to me.

It felt awkward. I wasn't prepared to talk to Anthony after such a long lapse in communication. I asked him if he could come over Thursday evening. He simply said yes and added, "Let me talk to Joe again."

Joseph just listened and nodded his head.

After Joseph put down the receiver, he turned to me, "Tony was in our back yard a couple nights ago, crying like a baby."

After a few more minutes, Joe and his wife walked me to the door. Over the years, I had been graciously entertained in their home many times, for holidays, their boys' birthdays and special gatherings. Yet I didn't know as I was leaving that I would never set foot in that house again. I had no conception of the magnitude of what was unfolding.

My meeting with Anthony was rescheduled for Saturday. Gina, feeling uneasy, decided to take Luke to a local park. Anthony arrived with his two sons, who kept themselves busy outside. I was alone with Anthony in a strangely formal and uncomfortable conversation.

"Can you tell me what happened?" I asked.

He seemed to glare at me for a minute before saying, "There's nothing to tell."

"Well," I replied, hesitantly, "what were you doing in that bank?"

"I don't really know," he said quickly and softly.

"Were you going to rob it?" I asked.

That made him angry. "Don't be ridiculous," he said, tersely.

"Do you remember being there?" I probed again.

"Let's just get this over with," he replied. "What can you do for me?"

"Well, I know this psychiatrist. . . . He's very good. Maybe he can help you."

I was worried he would be offended at that, but he actually perked up.

"You mean like a temporary insanity thing?" he asked.

"Well, that's possible," I said, scratching my head and looking at the floor. "I'm sure he can help you if you would be willing to see him."

We walked outside together. He leaned against his sports car. I told him how judges looked favorably on people who were trying to help themselves. I talked about the legal steps in a trial, but he seemed uninterested. Perhaps he had heard it already from his own attorney.

The psychiatrist's number was in my Rolodex at work, so we went to the juvenile facility. I talked into the outside speaker, went past the security checkpoint and took out my large set of keys to unlock the series of doors that led to my office. Anthony's boys waited in the car, but Tony came with me. As I was flipping for the number, he saw a pair of handcuffs on my desk.

"Do you know what it's like to have handcuffs on your wrists?" he asked defiantly.

I shook my head as I handed him the phone number.

I didn't realize as he drove out of the parking lot that we'd just had our last face-to-face conversation.

* * *

The following week my secretary at the juvenile facility said over the intercom, "Two gentlemen are here to see you."

I was puzzled. There was nothing in my appointment calendar, so I assumed they were salesmen. Vendors often came unsolicited.

I invited them into my office, and immediately both men produced FBI credentials.

"Have a seat," I said.

I wasn't surprised. The FBI visiting isn't all that unusual when you work in the criminal justice system.

"We're here to talk about your brothers," one agent said.

I was so shocked I didn't even notice he had said *brothers.* What did dawn on me was that banks are under federal jurisdiction. That would bring the FBI into Anthony's case.

Then the questions began. The first question was pointed. "What do you know about the crime?"

"All I know is that my brother told me he was arrested for trespassing."

I knew that the unadulterated truth would be the best policy, whether or not the agents would believe it.

"You can look at my bank records if you want," I told them. "You can come into my home without a search warrant. But frankly, I don't know anything."

I quickly got a better idea of what Anthony was accused of. On September 3, a customer at the First National Bank of Lake Forest, an affluent suburb of the north shore of Chicago, complained that a panel had fallen from a washroom ceiling. A maintenance man was putting it back in place when he saw a man in the crawlspace. He had the police called. Minutes later Lake Forest police, with their guns drawn, joined the bank security guard in the washroom. My brother Anthony was found crouched there in the false ceiling, which was adjacent to the safe-deposit vault. He had five screwdrivers, a jogging suit, pliers, two flashlights, a pair of scissors, gloves, an alarm clock, a radio and a bottle of water. Other tools were found, including an industrial-size jackhammer, bits and an electric saw.

One bank employee immediately recognized Anthony as a daily visitor to the safe-deposit vault. The FBI agents theorized that Anthony had visited often to bring more tools each time. They conjectured that he had planned to spend the weekend in the vault in order to rob it.

I sat there totally astonished. This was my brother, after all! It just wasn't possible. How could he get the knowledge to rob a bank or to break into a vault?

As hard as that was to believe, the news became more shocking.

One FBI agent continued, "We have reason to believe your brothers are involved in a series of bank burglaries."

"You said *brothers*," I said haltingly.

"Yes," the agent responded. "Both of your brothers are involved."

"That's not possible," I responded quickly. "I *know* Joe. He's been a barber and a salesman most of his life."

I'd just talked to him in his home, and he had acted totally surprised by Anthony's arrest. And even if he wanted to rob a bank, how could Joe manage it? He had a serious heart condition!

After a lengthy visit, the FBI left. For the longest time, I sat in my office looking out the window, feeling totally numb. It all seemed so unreal. We had known Italians who had committed crimes, but none were members of our own family.

I called my brother Joseph when I got home.

"I can't talk on the telephone," he said. I realized that he feared the phones were being tapped.

"The FBI said you were *both* involved," I asked him pointedly.

He responded, "Don't trust them. They're bad people. They're trying to solve all their unsolved cases by using our family."

His wife, on an extension phone, interjected, "You don't have to talk to them. Don't cooperate."

I called Anthony at home, but he didn't want to talk. I asked why he hadn't told me about all the burglary tools.

"I can't talk on the phone," he said and hung up.

Finally, I called my mother. She sounded terribly nervous and tearful. She told me that Joseph had said everything was going to be okay.

"But Mom," I interrupted, "he was caught in the ceiling of a bank."

"He's innocent," she screamed. "How can you believe your brother is a criminal?"

The conversation went downhill rapidly. She was determined beyond all logic to believe the best.

* * *

Several weeks later, two FBI agents came to my home.

Agent Heimbach said, "We believe your brothers have stolen more than two million dollars."

"Some money could be in a Swiss bank," the other agent said.

I remembered Anthony's trip to Switzerland. I started thinking about all the other trips, the changes of appearance, the conversations Joe and Anthony had together.

The FBI was interested in more than the bank in Lake Forest. They suspected that my brothers were responsible for the largest bank burglary in U.S. history.

The agent continued, "We think," he said, "on Saturday, April eleventh, Anthony used a credit card to get by a glass door leading to the vault at the First National Bank of Barrington. He then crawled on top of the safe-deposit boxes and dropped into a twenty-four-inch space in the corner. The bank employees didn't know the space existed. We don't know how *he* knew this. At one o'clock in the morning the vault's heavy metal door closed. It had a time lock, and would not open again until seven-thirty the next Monday morning. The Barrington police arrived when an alarm went off but found nothing suspicious. Ten minutes later, another alarm went off. The police returned again and turned it off, concluding that the alarm system wasn't working properly."

As they went on, I felt odd, as if I were listening to the story line of a movie that was about some stranger, not my brother. I had to force myself to understand.

The agents went on, "He then dropped into the vault area, drilled through locks and sawed off hinges, taking gems, jewelry, gold and cash, leaving behind bonds or paper. With the possibility of drug money being in some of the boxes, we will never know how much was there, but your brother got over a million dollars and maybe as much as two million. Nothing has been recovered."

They explained how Anthony had rented safe-deposit boxes at other banks as well, including the First National Bank of Lake Forest. Together with Joseph, they visited those boxes over sixty times. They had used phoney names, but Joseph's handwriting matched the false signature. The FBI believed that at the bank in Lake Forest, Joseph kept a bank employee busy while Anthony put tools in the false ceiling of the restroom and punched holes in the alarm system to disable it.

They further believed that Anthony intended to place an alarm clock in the ceiling, directly over the sensors, set to ring after the bank closed. The two of them would then sit in the van some distance from the bank, and when the police did not arrive, they would know the vault alarm wasn't working.

I still found it very difficult to believe Joseph was involved.

One agent added, "We think your brothers are connected with some subversive group to funnel money to terrorists in Central America or perhaps the Middle East."

That last comment shocked me. Now we were talking espionage or treason.

Where was this going to stop?

The next stop turned out to be prison for Anthony. While the FBI was still investigating federal charges, Anthony pleaded guilty to Illinois charges and received a three-and-a-half-year state sentence. Anthony went to a medium-security facility.

The federal officials were very clear. Unless the money was recovered, they would wait until the end of his state sentence and prosecute him on the federal charges.

During Anthony's prison term, my mother never admitted he was guilty, although he had pleaded guilty. She sometimes referred to him as a political prisoner. I began to take on the role of the black sheep of the family as my mother began implying that Anthony was some sort of Robin Hood, having taken the money from the rich to help me with Luke's medical bills.

I resented it and told my family so. And the distance between us widened.

After a year and a half, Anthony was released. The family had a large homecoming party to which Gina and I were not invited.

For a while, communication, although minimal, continued. Luke would get Christmas presents from Joseph and his wife, and his cousins would talk to him at least once a year on the telephone, but that was all. Things were strained to the limit, I thought. But I was wrong. Things would get worse.

Chapter 12

WITNESS FOR THE PROSECUTION

B Y THE TIME ANTHONY WAS RELEASED FROM STATE PRISON I WAS
working at the Billy Graham Center. One day, the FBI
called again. While my brother was in prison, the federal
prosecutor's office had continued their investigation.
"The federal prosecutor would like you to come downtown
and talk with him," the agent said.

I went to the prosecutor's office in downtown Chicago. He
informed me that they were going ahead with their case and
intended to prosecute both of my brothers on federal charges.

Since the time Anthony had been convicted on the state level
of attempted burglary and conspiring to commit burglary at the
First National Bank of Lake Forest (the bank where he'd been
caught in the ceiling), the FBI had found other banks in which
my brother had safe-deposit boxes and had made numerous
trips; they each had the type of security system that could be
disarmed with an ice pick.

One such bank was only several feet from the Velvet Brush

Beauty Shop, which Anthony owned and was then living in. There had been a robbery attempt there in 1979.

According to the prosecutor, my brother Anthony crept into the bushes behind the Deerfield bank on Sunday, July 22, 1979. He had a large supply of equipment, including crowbars, two sledge-hammers, a torch and a headlamp. He supposedly unscrewed a ventilation cover and dropped into a room adjacent to the safe-deposit vault. The prosecutor said that my brother was drilling into the wall when a janitor, who had heard some noises, entered the basement conference room and discovered Anthony standing on a chair. There was plaster and concrete everywhere.

The prosecutor believed he bluffed his way out by yelling at the janitor, "Who is going to clean up this mess?"

The janitor, believing Anthony was a repairman, rushed off, but by the time he came back with a broom, Anthony was gone, having left behind the tools and an unfinished hole in the wall.

Another of Anthony's suspected targets was the First National Bank of Barrington, the site of the largest bank burglary in the history of America. The case remained unsolved. My brother not only had a safe-deposit box there, but both of my brothers, according to the FBI, visited the bank fifty times prior to the burglary.

Is there no end to this?

Then the prosecutor asked me, "Did your brothers ever offer you a large sum of money?"

"My brothers offered me fifty thousand dollars to start a camera store."

At the time I had no idea how that brief answer would affect the rest of my life.

"Do you recall the date?" the prosecutor asked quickly.

Because our little walk outside coincided with a family function, the date was still in my mind—April 19, 1979. Anthony's comments played through my mind once more: "We've had some luck in business recently," referring to himself and Joseph.

The prosecutor looked grimly gratified. "The First National Bank of Barrington was robbed six days before that offer—on April 12."

Then something still more unexpected came. He said he intended to subpoena me to testify before a grand jury.

"I do not want to testify," I said flatly.

"Your brothers and your family won't be there," he said. "I would never have you testify in a trial. I rarely have somebody testify in front of his own family, unless he's an eyewitness."

What little I knew was circumstantial, but the prosecutor still wanted my testimony because he was trying to piece a case together.

Several months later, I received his subpoena. I now had no choice but to arrive as requested at the Dirksen Federal Building. The prosecutor and FBI agents were waiting. One of the agents said, "This has got to be really difficult, but remember, your brothers are adults. They knew what they were doing, and they've got to pay the consequences."

That all made sense, but it was still hard to live with the fact that I might be helping to convict them. I couldn't understand how God would use this situation. After everything else, to ask me to be a witness against my own family seemed too much. But I had no choice.

All too soon I sat before the grand jury. After preliminary questions I was asked if I had direct knowledge of the bank burglaries of Barrington, Lake Forest or Deerfield.

Each time I said no.

Then they asked me if my brothers had ever offered me a large sum of money. I paused for the longest time. Having been in many courtrooms, I knew there were ways to avoid a question. One could be forgetful. Frequently, over the years I heard, "I can't recall."

I just couldn't do that. I cleared my throat and said, "Yes."

One of the jurors asked, "There are only three brothers in your family, and two of them are involved in burglary. You really didn't know anything?"

When I said no, several jurors in the back whispered to each other and laughed. Their laughter really upset me. I realized for the first time that there would be those who would assume I was involved, partly because Italians have a reputation for organized crime, but mostly I'm sure because it seemed inconceivable that two brothers could be deeply involved in anything without the third knowing something.

After my testimony was over, I was ushered out of the room. I had never learned what else the grand jury would see in terms of evidence or witnesses, so I had no idea what effect my testimony would have or what the jurors would decide. I returned home to await their decision.

A week later an FBI agent called me.

"Have you heard the news? Both of your brothers have been indicted on seven counts of bank burglary and conspiracy."

Several radio shows covered the story, as well as some local papers, but it still seemed so unreal. I hoped my part in the sad affair was over. But many months later, I received a federal subpoena for the trial.

I couldn't believe my eyes. It wasn't possible! The prosecutor had assured me I would never be called to a trial to be a prosecution witness against my own family.

Shaking as I dialed the phone, I called him immediately and said, "What *is* this?"

"We need your testimony for the trial," the prosecutor said calmly.

"But it's circumstantial," I retorted. "You *don't* need it!"

"That's your opinion," he said. "I believe we need it."

"Don't you understand?" I responded. "You're expecting me to repeat my testimony in front of my mother and brothers and other members of my family!"

"I know it will be difficult," he said, "but we do need it."

"I don't think I can do it," was my response.

He quickly became tougher. "You have a subpoena. There's no choice. If you disregard it, you'll be held in contempt of court."

Why did God allow me to get caught in this squeeze play?

I didn't understand. I'd been a court officer for years and had upheld the law. Now I could face a fine or jail for disregarding a subpoena. How could I make exceptions for my own family without ruining my credibility?

While I wasn't happy with the prosecutor's office, my real anger was directed toward my brothers. They had dragged me into something that had become a Catch-22—either I incur the wrath of the family or the wrath of the court. I realized that my brothers were probably overwhelmed by their own problems, but I wished they could have thought of me too. There hadn't been so much as an apology from anyone to me or my wife for dragging our family into such trouble. I suppose what I was looking for was not so much a confession but something like, "We can't give you any details, but we're sorry you got dragged into this." I never heard that; I never heard anything.

The trial date fell during a three-day trip I had scheduled to train court officers in Aurora, Illinois. I decided to go through with the first and last day and drive back to Chicago in between.

I was quite tired when I returned to my hotel room after the first day of lecturing. I looked at the subpoena next to the telephone. I read it again, and at about ten o'clock that night, after a lot of thinking and rationalization, I made the decision not to appear. I didn't think I could handle it emotionally. I called Gina and told her.

She said, "Whatever you think is best, I'm behind you."

"Even if it means a fine or going to jail?" I asked.

"You have got to do what you think is right. You know God will help you no matter what you decide to do," she replied.

"I know that," I responded.

I turned out the light but was unable to sleep. I was startled some time later by the phone ringing. It was about midnight. I wondered if Gina were having second thoughts.

But it wasn't Gina. It was the federal prosecutor.

"Sorry to call you so late," he said. "I heard the weather might be bad tomorrow, and I'm a little concerned you might not get here on time. I decided to send several FBI agents to your hotel to pick you up."

I said very little before he hung up. Then I got out of bed and looked out the window. It felt as if I were under arrest, having agents come to escort me.

Suddenly it hit me. How did he know where I was? I'd left no forwarding number. My home phone was tapped!

The next morning was foggy, but I could see the government car in the parking lot. One of the agents got out. He stayed in my room while I dressed. After I got into the car, he handed me a copy of my testimony before the grand jury.

"You may want this to refresh your memory."

I didn't need to refresh my memory. It was all too clear.

When we arrived at the location of the courtroom, another agent joined us. They sat next to me in the waiting area. I saw family members pass down the hall, but one by one they would look the other way. Then, for the first time in two years, I saw my brother Anthony. He was walking down the hall to a small room. He never looked in my direction.

I learned that Joseph had been separated from the trial, which meant his part was being postponed because of his health. Although indicted as a co-conspirator, his heart condition kept him from standing trial.

Unknown to me, several colleagues at the Billy Graham Center, led by Dr. Mel Lorentzen, were even then forming a prayer circle around my desk, praying for two things: that I would not have to appear and that I would not have to testify. As I waited my turn, I half wondered if something would happen so that my testimony would not be needed. But at the same time I wondered whether God had a greater—if more painful—plan.

The wait was long—several hours. Then suddenly an agent approached me quickly and said, "You're wanted in the courtroom."

With one agent on either side of me, I was brought to the door of the large, modern courtroom. The room was filled to capacity; many people were forced to stand in the back. Courtrooms like this were so familiar to me. I had testified hundreds of times over the years, but this was so different. My stomach was in knots, and the whole experience seemed like a bad dream.

An agent pointed in the direction of the witness box and said,

"The rest of the way you'll have to walk alone."

It was really a short distance from the doors to the witness box, but I felt as if I were dragging a cross.

I sat in the witness box and looked over at my brother Anthony sitting behind the defense table. He looked pale and sullen, his eyes downcast. I glanced up quickly to see my mother and other family members. Then I saw my pastor, Bob Harvey, who had been nearby during my other "trials." Bob's sticking with me seemed really important. Seeing him gave me a renewed sense of God's presence.

I had never heard the swearing-in phrase quite the way I did that day.

The bailiff said, "Do you swear to tell the truth, the whole truth and nothing but the truth, so help you God?"

"I do," I replied firmly.

As the prosecutor began leafing through several pages of a long legal pad, I looked around the courtroom quickly. There were two long tables with exhibits—tools, gloves and the like, confiscated from the two burglary attempts. There were also large charts which I didn't have time to read.

He asked me my name and occupation for the record, then asked me to point out my brother and identify an article of clothing he was wearing. The simple gesture of pointing at Anthony was the first contact we had had in several years. He looked up, and our eyes met briefly.

The prosecutor moved right to the question, "Did your brother Anthony ever offer you a large sum of money?"

"Yes," I responded.

When I said things from the stand that were incriminating, I tried to say them quietly, but it never worked. The more I tried to be quiet, the more the judge would tell me to speak up and lean into the microphone.

At the conclusion of the testimony, Anthony's defense attorney made his cross-examination. I looked over at my brother again.

Sitting in the witness box, I felt as if I were in another dimension. *My God!* I said to myself, *This is my brother. We slept in the*

same bed together growing up. He held my hand walking to
church when I was small. He brought me to Saturday-matinee
movies. How can a relationship end like this?

I realized that the defense attorney intended to discredit me
as a witness. The first issue was the money my brother gave me
to help with those mortgage payments during one of Luke's surgeries. Now it became a loan which, according to the attorney,
I had refused to repay. Next, he tried to attack my memory for
any of Anthony's travels or physical changes by asking what dress
my wife had worn to a Fourth of July party. Of course I couldn't
remember.

A recess was called after which I was to continue my testimony.
My brother hurried into a small room off the courtroom. I briefly
saw the back of his head as I walked down the hall.

The worst part of the trial was the churning ambivalence, that
pendulum of emotion swinging from the extreme anger, to the
love and compassion I felt. Which was the right feeling? I realize
now as I look back that they were both authentic. That is what
made it so difficult. I realize too that what I felt toward my brother
during that trial is exactly what I'd felt toward my father growing
up: ambivalence . . . getting stuck emotionally . . . trying to love
someone and to dislike his behavior all at once.

And I suppose, reflecting back, Anthony felt the same ambivalence toward me. I'm sure he felt a brother's love toward me and
deep pain that now I was helping the prosecution to send him
to prison.

I returned to the witness stand. This time I began looking at
the jury, a group of total strangers. I even felt anger toward them
and the spectators. Were they enjoying the testimony as they
would some kind of soap opera?

I wished that the trial had been a bench trial before the judge
alone. These were very personal things I was talking about, my
relationship with my brothers. But now a private family matter was
very much a public spectacle. It surely was even harder on my
mother, with her Sicilian tradition of privacy and family secrets.

At the end of my testimony I was informed that I had to return the next day for more cross-examination by my brother's attorney. I had wanted this to be over quickly, but now the tension would remain.

The FBI agent driving me back to Aurora said, "Let's stop and have dinner." He chose an Italian restaurant.

Curious about his background, I asked him why he had decided to become an FBI agent.

He said, "I looked up to my brother who was an FBI agent. He was killed in the line of duty."

"How did it happen?" I asked.

He looked at me and said, "He arrived at the scene of a bank robbery, and the bank robber shot him."

The next day I was allowed to drive myself to the court. The defense attorney began his cross-examination by trying to get me angry. Using some of my wedding pictures as part of the court record, he held up one particular picture of my brother Anthony holding a glass of wine.

"Can you identify the person in the photograph?" he asked.

"Yes, that's my brother Tony."

"And what is he doing in this photograph?" he asked further.

"He's proposing a toast at my wedding. He was my best man."

Then with a sweeping motion, he took the photograph and held it in front of the jury.

"And how is it that several years ago he was your best man, and today you are doing this to him?"

If he was trying to get me mad, he succeeded. I had to battle with myself not to show it.

As a parting shot, he tried a new line of questioning—my mother's favorite "Robin Hood" idea that Anthony had stolen money to help me pay for Luke's medical bills. And with that, I was excused.

I will never forget walking out of that courtroom. There were no agents, not even the prosecutor to say thank you or good-by. I walked down a Chicago street, thinking about the Civil War and that I understood now how brothers could end up on different sides of a conflict. But I knew I was not angry at God, even though

I was questioning the whole affair. I didn't understand how he would use this, but I understood clearly who was responsible. I hung on to the simple belief that followers of Christ were not to lie. Although I had witnessed a lot of untruthfulness on the witness stand over the years, I had no choice but to take that oath seriously.

Bob Harvey did more than anyone to help me after the trial. Many times, I would ask him if I had sounded vindictive or had spilled my guts to hurt my family. Again and again he reassured me that it looked very painful and that I had given minimal answers.

When I returned home that evening, I looked through a family album. I came upon a picture of my brother holding my hand. I must have been about three or four years old.

In my mind I said to the picture, *I trusted you. Why did you do this?*

When my father died, I had felt there would be more peace in the family, but now there was far more tension than at any time while he was alive.

Monday morning, an FBI agent called me. "The jury has just returned a verdict. Your brother was found guilty of six of the seven counts."

I could feel my heart racing.

Then he added, "The prosecution is asking for the maximum—fifty-five years in prison."

Chapter 13

AFTERMATH

A FTER THE FBI AGENT HUNG UP, I SAT AT MY DESK AND STARED vacantly out the window for the longest time, until I abruptly decided to call my mother.

"Did you hear the verdict?" I asked.

Her response was not unexpected. Everything would be okay, she said, because Joseph had assured her there would be an appeal and Anthony would get off.

"Mother," I said, "Anthony has been in state prison, and now he will go to a federal one."

"You didn't have to testify!" she all but screamed back.

Now for the first time, I tried to explain about the subpoena, how I had no choice, how I had to tell the truth under oath; it did no good.

"He's innocent! He's innocent!" she kept protesting.

"He was found with burglary tools in the ceiling of a bank."

She dismissed it lightly.

I retorted, "Your son committed a crime. Both Anthony and Joseph lied to you."

"You think you're so holy," she said, "working for Billy Graham and going to churches. Well, you're nothing but a hypocrite! You don't care about your family. You're a Judas. I guess I don't have three sons anymore. I just have two sons."

I shouldn't have done it, but I hung up on her. I took a deep breath and leaned back to gaze out my window at the collegiate halls across the way, so sturdy, so solid. I felt anything but sturdy and solid at that moment.

I had always thought the worst part would be testifying, but I was wrong. This—the aftermath—was worse. I talked to my mother over the phone many more times, but our relationship became even more difficult and strained. Calls often escalated into arguments.

Looking back, I realize we were living in two different worlds. My mother was what she had always been, a product of our mutual ancestry, in a place, actually, I would be today if customs and family tradition were inescapable. From the time she was a child, my mother had learned to look at the best traits of people and block out their shady business dealings or criminal activities. That was why she could concentrate on what a good and sensitive father Tony was and deny the rest. By trying to defend my own position, I cast myself in the impossible situation of convincing a mother that her son was a criminal when she refused to see it.

Two weeks after the jury's verdict, Anthony appeared before the federal judge, Marvin Aspen, for sentencing. His defense attorney worked hard to keep him out of prison by pointing to the nonviolent nature of the crime.

The U.S. attorney called my brother "a hairdresser with a secret life. . . . He became a vault burglar, the first person in U.S. history to gain entry to and rob a bank safe-deposit vault."

Even the judge and the prosecutors seemed to have mixed opinions about my brother. He might be a "common criminal," but as the prosecutor put it, he was "probably the most brilliant burglar in the country." The FBI agents seemed to admire the skill with which he committed the crimes. The prosecutor even called Anthony a "criminal genius. . . . The first man to spend a weekend in a bank safe-deposit vault and walk out with a million dollars."

But Anthony did not take any bows that Tuesday morning; he

maintained his innocence. Judge Aspen made it clear that he did not believe my brother. He was willing to consider a sentence reduction if there was cooperation in the return of lost money and valuables, but the judge dismissed any notion that Anthony would receive a short prison sentence and thereafter enjoy the money he had hidden.

Anthony was sentenced to twenty years in prison, a $25,000 fine and five years' probation after the prison sentence. It was a harsh sentence. I knew prisoners across America who had received half that sentence for involuntary manslaughter and other violent crimes. Immediately, Anthony was handcuffed by federal marshalls and brought across town to the Federal Metropolitan Correctional Center in Chicago.

Joseph remained at home, convalescing from heart surgery, but he remained under the cloud of indictment as a co-conspirator. If Joseph was involved, as the federal indictment indicated, it was clear now that Anthony was taking the rap for the two of them; he wasn't talking.

Right after the sentencing, Anthony's photograph appeared on the front page of the *Chicago Tribune,* and other stories ran in the *Chicago Sun-Times* and smaller local papers. A *Chicago Tribune* reporter, Maurice Posely, said, "It is a tale of steeled nerves, gall, and a cunning criminal mind. It was a meticulously planned crime, which called for intelligence and a cool-headness."

Normally, I don't notice newspapers lying around, but on March 4, 1985, things were different. I saw the *Chicago Tribune,* with its photograph of Anthony and the headline "BANK JOB A PERFECT JOB—ALMOST," everywhere. In the Graham Library. On a colleague's desk. In a self-serve paper vender. At the drugstore. Beside the cash register at the gas station.

I knew it was time to tell Luke. He was almost eight, and I couldn't keep from him something that the whole community and his classmates could read about for themselves. Luke would not see his uncle for a long time, nor perhaps other family members, and he would need to know why.

I sat him down and explained the difference between right and wrong, which he understood. I told him that Uncle Tony was locked in prison and that he wouldn't see him for a long time. He went into his bedroom for quite a while and then came out with a crayoned picture of Jesus in the boat with his disciples.

"I'll send this picture to Uncle Tony," Luke said, "because he needs Jesus in his heart."

The child had cut through to the essence of the matter. While I was preoccupied with Anthony's crime against society, and my family was preoccupied with getting my brother's sentence reduced, the important thing had always been whether or not Uncle Tony had Jesus in his heart.

More and more I felt a new sense of God's grace; if God hadn't brought certain people and circumstances into my life, I easily could have been part of all my brothers did and all my family had come to think of as the only acceptable life.

By his grace, God had driven me in a very different direction. My new ministry gave me the opportunity to be with the attorney general, the highest law-enforcement official in the land, and with Norman Carlson, the head of the Federal Bureau of Prisons. Essentially, they were my brother's keepers.

After my persecution from the warden and the intimation from the head of the probation department that I would never get anywhere in the court system, I found myself in a historic room in the U.S. Supreme Court, sitting with the chief justice. It came during his seventeenth year as chief justice, only months before his retirement. I remember clearly walking in the marble hallways and beneath the large, white columns, all the while thinking what a great privilege this was for a kid from Austin Avenue. Most attorneys will never argue a case before the Supreme Court, no less sit with the chief justice.

Clearly when God has a plan, nothing can stand in his way, and although many thought for sure my days in the judicial and correctional system had come to an end, great triumphs were yet to come.

Yet my love and concern for Tony sometimes made my job difficult emotionally. To avoid confrontation, I stayed clear of the prisons Anthony was in. Even so, more than once, I'd think I'd see his face among the prisoners in the hundred prisons I've visited across the country.

I knew I couldn't use any influence I might have to improve Anthony's situation. The only thing I felt comfortable doing was finding out where Tony would be. At one point I learned that Anthony was being transferred to a new prison in Milan, Michigan. Sometime later I asked an evangelist going to the Michigan prison to share Christ with Anthony but not to use my name. The evangelist told me afterward, "Your brother is a very angry man."

One day the FBI informed me that some of the jewelry had been returned. The judge was willing to reduce the sentence, but after careful examination at the FBI lab, the jewelry turned out to be counterfeit. Then almost a year later, Anthony's attorney gave the FBI a million dollars worth of jewelry and heirlooms. According to my mother, "It just turned up." This time after the FBI examination, it proved to be authentic and showed signs of having been submerged in water. I remember what mixed emotions I had at the news—sad that Tony was guilty and relieved to know he indeed *had* lied to me and everyone.

I'd been very close to my mother for many years, and so this separation in later life was painful for both of us. As the years went by, my relationship with her became more distressing. I could not discuss my ministry, because the words *jail* or *prison* upset her. Because she maintained that Anthony was innocent, my testimony would ever seem to her an evil deed. The unpardonable sin, according to Sicilian tradition, was betrayal of a family member. Gina and I were banished from family events.

Several weeks after the trial, Gina had received a package containing all our presents to Tony's family over the years. The message of rejection was obvious. Even after Anthony went to prison, he exerted influence from his cell, insisting we should not be invited to family events. I continued writing to Anthony. The message was always the same: "No matter what you think of us, we will not stop loving you or praying for you." He never answered.

It was inevitable, of course, that some event would bring us together with the family. In 1986, one of my cousins died. Though my mother tried to keep us from the funeral by withholding the details, we found out the location and showed up. The tension was obvious in everybody's face as Gina and I walked in and sat several rows behind the others. My mother sat squarely between her other daughters-in-law.

At the end of the service, Gina said, "Let's say hello to them."

That was not what was on my mind, but I followed her lead. One by one, family members turned their backs on us, put their hands in their pockets and walked away. Several nodded at Gina briefly, but the wives, and Joseph especially, ignored me. I tapped one of my nephews on the shoulder, and he shrugged away.

Though it hurt, I could see how they were only doing a normal thing, even the right thing, according to their heritage. I regret that my mother's childhood world turned into a dysfunctional marriage and that my brother's crime so devastated her. I understood how, from her world view and background, she saw family unity as the most important value.

I still love each of my family members deeply, and fervently hope that they will be saved. Perhaps then there will be reconciliation and reunion.

Many times in the years that followed, I've asked myself if given the same set of circumstances (subpoenas to a grand jury and to a trial, and swearing under oath to tell the truth), I would testify again. The answer would be yes.

When I entered a personal relationship with Jesus in the corn field, I had no idea what the ramifications were. I wouldn't have wanted to know that it could lead to separation from my own family. Ironically, following Christ has created some of the hardest situations in my life. I think now I understand better the meaning of taking up your cross. I had always wanted the cross to be something more manageable, something that I was willing to take on. In my own life, the cross has proven to be precisely what I did not want, often what would hurt the most.

I found comfort in God's Word and ministering for him. And

I came to appreciate more and more the larger family he had given me—Gina and Luke, Gloria and Bill Beyers, Bob Harvey and the rest of the family of God.

Gina and I especially needed comfort from our "family" when, in 1987, we found that Luke needed a third open-heart surgery. I learned at this point in my life to be honest with God. Consequently I experienced the heights of joy and fear. And I marveled how God was working in our son's life. He was very brave, reassuring Gina and me through the process. It amazed me how God's grace touched him.

Luke later told of the experience when, at age twelve, he made his confession of faith before the elders and pastor of our church. When the elders asked Luke what the church meant to him, Luke talked about his third open-heart surgery. The elders and the pastor were close to tears when Luke related the story of how a surgical nurse offered him a puppet or a stuffed toy to take with him on the surgery cart but that he decided what he wanted most was his Bible. God had already been speaking to him.

And the ordeal confirmed for me that my old theology was no longer part of my life. Before Luke went into surgery, a woman said to me, "If you pray hard enough, your son's heart will be healed."

I would have believed that years before, but now I knew that it was not a formula that got God's attention.

In many ways, this surgery to replace a valve in Luke's heart was the most difficult and yet the one with the most blessings. When we needed fresh blood for the surgery, sixty people signed up, ten of whom came to the hospital before six o'clock in the morning.

During a crucial moment after the surgeons had replaced the valve, a nurse entered the waiting room.

She said, "We have a problem here."

Everyone was silent.

"His heart isn't responding," she continued.

I felt a chill and a terrible sinking feeling. The interval before the next report was filled with anxiety. I realized that there was a possibility that Luke would never wake up from the surgery, yet I put my trust in God. Twenty minutes later, at 1:05 P.M., we received the joyous news that Luke's heart was pumping. Doctors had assisted with drugs to help with the contractions. As before, Pastor Harvey was there to share in the good news.

Then, in a matter of twenty-four hours, we saw what a nurse called "accelerated healing." Although normally it takes a week for these steps to take place, the breathing tube was quickly removed, then the arterial lines were removed, then the chest tube was removed, and finally Luke's eyes popped open in response to Gina's voice. Only two days after the lengthly open-heart surgery, Luke was walking the hospital corridors. Pastor Harvey shared the joyous news with our church.

At one point, a nurse entered our room and was puzzled by a list that looked like a political petition.

"It's a prayer list," I responded, but I could see he did not understand.

"Well, if it makes you feel better," he responded.

"It has nothing to do with how we feel," I told him. "Look at how well Luke is doing. That's the power of prayer."

God certainly has a way of making up for difficulties in life. While my family did not come to visit Luke in the hospital, Luke received hundreds of letters from across the country because a national Christian radio station had kept their listeners informed. Luke's class at Wheaton Christian Grammar School prayed for him every day, and his teacher and principal came to visit. No, it wasn't any easier stopping at those surgery doors and watching our son being wheeled away, but we felt God's presence and the presence of his people.

In reviewing the last forty years of my life, I can see there have been a lot of valleys and a lot of pain. I've come to see that illness or accidents don't bring anywhere near the pain a broken relationship does. Yet I've come to understand that relationships won't be perfect. Broken promises don't surprise me anymore. I know that people will let you down, even betray you; but all of this has made me rely even more on God.

I still thank God for the family and the ethnic origin he chose for me. I am proud to be an Italian. I have so many fond memories of relatives who were warm and compassionate and filled with joy. But I can't help being reminded that my ancestry includes extremes: I have roots from an ancient and sophisticated civilization, and perhaps a trace of blood from Florentine artists and philosophers and Roman lawmakers. I may also have blood from Sicilian mafioso and perhaps the Roman soldiers who stood beneath the cross of Christ.

I've led a number of lives, really: a life of self-justifying legalism before I encountered Christ, and a new life after he became my Savior and Lord; a life of celibacy, and a happy married life; a life within my Sicilian family, and a life in the greater family of God. All of them were real; all were used by God in a greater plan.

Throughout my lives, God pursued me. That is very, very clear. And he kept pursuing me, never letting me alone, even when I wished he would. Through highs and lows that were great and horrific, through the inner city and into hospital waiting rooms, through self-righteous seminary days, through unemployment and wavering faith. Through life and death in a Texas forest, to prisons and courtrooms and a family torn apart by fundamental lies and truths.

If God has shown me anything, he has shown me that we do not have to be locked into the traditions of our culture or our families. But he has also shown me that choosing a better way does not constitute an easier way. Much of the pain I've known has come precisely from choosing to follow his way.

But always, through it all, God has kept pursuing me. And that has made it possible to keep choosing him.

Epilog

In 1985, I was a delegate to the United Nations Conference on the Treatment of Offenders. The conference offered me my first trip to the land of my ancestors, Italy.

While in Rome, I planned a visit to the Vatican, not as a pilgrim but as a student of history. Ever since I'd met God not in a marble sanctuary but in a corn field, churches—even the ultimate church—did not hold the same magical allure.

One warm, sunny morning, Gina and I rode the hotel bus down the Via Appia Antica, headed for the Vatican. I first caught sight of the Piazza San Pietro through the massive columns built by Bernini. I saw glimpses of the facade of St. Peter's Basilica through the hundreds of doric columns. Immediately my mind filled with the pictures my mother had shared with me as I grew up, pictures of the square jammed with thousands of faithful pilgrims. In actuality, it seemed just as large, but more magnificent than any image I had seen.

Gina and I walked to the basilica entrance, where two Swiss guards in ornate orange-and-blue uniforms stood solemnly. Striking white light was shafting down from the great dome. The baldachino (canopy) over the main altar was a brilliant bronze.

Beside it were colossal statues of the four doctors of the church. I was captivated by the artistry of Michelangelo, Raphael, Rubens and Leonardo da Vinci.

The sight of statues and candles, the smell of incense and the sound of Latin hit me full force. The old quest for the hidden, the unknown came flooding back.

Suddenly, I found myself choked with emotion, tears welling in my eyes. In that moment many pieces of my life came together.

So much of God had been a mystery to me growing up, and yet some of his mystery still remained. I still did not understand why God had pursued me so vigilantly. Even so, I was sure he had worked a great work in my life. Through his grace, my early dreams had *not* come true. The person standing in the center of St. Peter's Basilica was not the strutting cardinal I once planned to become but, rather, a very different man.

Even without fame and fortune, the life God planned for me was better than any dream I'd dreamed. I loved God! His Son, Jesus Christ, was my Savior and friend! I no longer needed to find my security in legalism, ceremony and church law. How grateful I was that God had been patient with me.

I remembered all my prayers for suffering as a young seminarian who thought suffering would draw him closer to God. Perhaps God had answered those prayers too. At last I was following the advice of my old spiritual director, Father Howland; I no longer prayed for suffering. But I could see how God had used it in my life all the same.

As I left the basilica, I saw the image on a crucifix and was filled with joy. I now knew the man on the cross, and I knew what he had done for me.

You hold me by my right hand. You guide me with your counsel, and afterward you will take me into glory. Whom have I in heaven but you? And earth has nothing I desire besides you. (Ps 73:23-25)